Step Zero II: Preparation for a SCUBA Live-Aboard Trip

**Dennis Adams   Chuck McCown
Cathy Swan   Peter Swan**

Step Zero II: Preparation for a
SCUBA Live-Aboard Trip

Copyright © 2009 by:
Dennis Adams, Chuck McCown,
Cathy W. Swan, & Peter A. Swan

All rights reserved, including the rights to reproduce
this manuscript or portions thereof in any form.

Published by SouthWest Analytic Network, Inc.
dr-swan@cox.net

ISBN 978-0-578-01943-7

Printed in the United States of America

TABLE OF CONTENTS

PREFACE V

CHAPTER 1: INTRODUCTION TO STEP ZERO 1
- Step Zero: Getting Started on a SCUBA Photo Trip 2
- Setting Expectations 4

CHAPTER 2: LIVE-ABOARD STRENGTHS "VALET DIVING" 7
- Live-Aboard Experiences 7
- Common Traits of a SCUBA Live-Aboard 8
- Typical Day -- Typical Scenario 12

CHAPTER 3: MAXIMUM ENJOYMENT FROM PLANNING 15
- Introduction 15
- Schedules & Checklists 16
- Travel Health 21
- Secure Electronic Storage for Lost Documents 24

CHAPTER 4: A LIVE-ABOARD ADVENTURE: A NOVICE'S VIEW 29
- Introduction 29
- Trip Preparation 29

CHAPTER 5: A LIVE-ABOARD EXAMPLE: SECOND SAILING OF THE PARADISE DANCER 35
- Preparation for the Trip 35
- Pre-Sailing Activities 37
- Top Dive Spots 43

CHAPTER 6: PREPARATION FOR UNDERWATER PHOTOGRAPHY 47
- Introduction 47
- Equipment Preparation 52
- Test Procedure (TP) 55
- Preparing for First Camera Dive: 58
- First Camera Dive 61
- After the Dive 65
- Saving your photos 66
- Getting Ready for your Next Photo Dive 67
- Flooded Camera – What to Do? 68

- Diving is done 69
- End of trip Check list 71
- Reminders for the Photo Pro 71
- Conclusion 72

CHAPTER 7: PLANNING FOR ONBOARD ENJOYMENT 75

- Introduction 75
- Leisure Time Expectation 76
- Personal Expectations 78
- Special Events on Land 79
- Special Events Underwater 80
- Cultural Events 81

CHAPTER 8: THE NEXT STEPS 83

- On the Way Home – Prep for Next Trip 83
- Deciding to Go 84
- Beginning Step Zero Again 85

APPENDIX: UNDERWATER PHOTO SAFARI CHECKLIST 87

- IMPORTANT - You MUST TAKE these following items!!!!! 88
- These are ACTIONS you must do 89
- Action Things to do ON the trip 95
- Action Things to do at the END of the trip 96
- Action Things to NOT take on the trip 97
- Equipments Check List 98

PREFACE

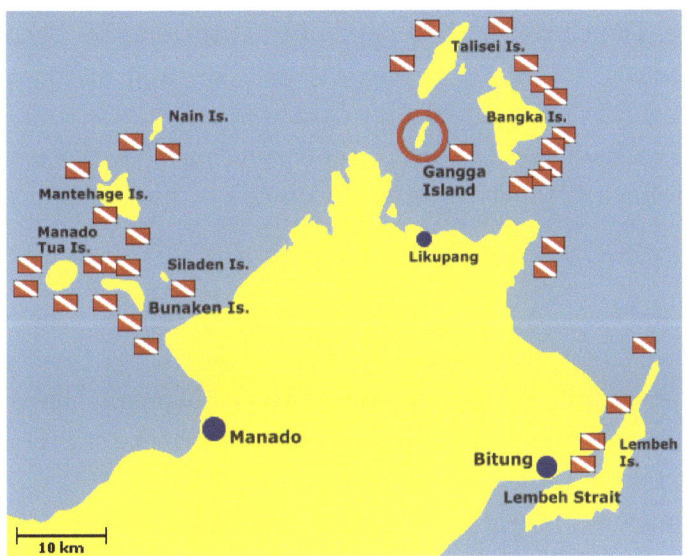

Step Zero II Book Purpose:
To help you prepare for an underwater photo safari on a live aboard!

The challenge of undertaking an Underwater Photo Safari is exhilarating and just plain fun. Each of us starts our adventures with different expectations and personal hopes. Each of us begin our trips with different preparation steps; and, frequently realize that we need help getting to the initial "kick-off" on this adventure of a lifetime. A SCUBA live aboard trip to some exotic location is truly an opportunity to reach out and have fun in a way that day to day activities do not allow. When we went looking for North Sulawesi, after reading about the Peter Hughes boat supporting northern Indonesia, we were captivated by that area of the world. The map [North Sulawesi – From: www.ganggaisland.com] shows the location, if not the beauty of those far distant lands. In the old days, travelers would spend months, if not years, to travel and experience what we were embarking on for three weeks. Air travel, inter-island transportation and modern communications enabled our team to experience those remarkable adventures that others only dreamed of.

The book we have written provides guidance toward solving the real problem of getting ready for the adventure of a lifetime. The checklist at the end of the book enables the traveler to better prepare for a truly massive excursion. The words, pictures, examples, and memorable experiences will help put the checklist into perspective for the reader and will show how and when to use it. You will minimize the likelihood of problems and assist in their solutions. The bottom line is that preparation, preparation, and preparation are the best ways to ensure a fun and successful underwater photo safari on a live aboard.

The authors of this book would like to thank the many people who helped us along the way. This would include those wonderful individuals who helped us in the air, on the boats, in the cars and in the hotels. These professionals around the world work every day, and hopefully, recognize that the travelers who pass by are on their trips of a lifetime and appreciate greatly the work that they do. One set of people who really make a difference are the ones who help us during the 16 hour airplane rides over vast expanses of the oceans of this world. They may not recognize how much they help our spirit as well as our stomachs and sleep clocks. Another key set of professionals, who we always appreciate, are the food handlers and the servers. We are able to reward them directly; but, we forget to tell them how much their friendly approaches help the wandering SCUBA diver a long way from home.

In addition, we would like to thank the Peter Hughes staff and the crew onboard the Paradise Dancer. Their assistance to just get to the ship is remarkable and necessary for those gargantuan trips around the world. The staff on the ship was great and the dive trip would not be nearly as successful and fulfilling without the cheerful assistance in all things onboard.

And then, of course, there is the thanks to the families who allow us to take these tremendous adventures around the world.

Thanks Cathy, Thanks Pete, Thanks Gail, Thanks Beth. We, the authors will explain quickly who we are: All four of us work in the field of rocket science. Cathy is our chief editor while Peter is the drafter of words and working editor. Dennis (fills out the team from our first book) produces the appropriate photo's, and creates the checklists. Both Pete and Dennis create the words, debate about content and finalize the presentation. Chuck is the new one to our crew; but, he has five decades of photography expertise and travel experiences. This team hopes to provide a book that is enjoyable to read and productive in preparing the reader for an underwater photo safari on a live aboard.

Chapter 1: Introduction to Step Zero

*Step Zero II Book Purpose:
To help you prepare for an underwater
photo safari on a live aboard!*

When choosing to go on an adventure, the choices are varied, extensive, complex, and sometimes intimidating. This mix of concerns will be addressed with the hope that your future trips will be rewarding and full of adventure and excitement. We will describe our joint adventure of SCUBA diving in the Coral Triangle on the Peter Hughes three mast schooner – Paradise Dancer. The extensive underwater photographic opportunities enabled us to really relax and concentrate on enjoying the remarkable congruence of circumstances – a new boat, a relatively new area of SCUBA exploration, and multiple friends experiencing it with us. To punctuate the message in this book, Dennis, Pete and Cathy prepared for their trip using the methods in their first book: **Step Zero: Getting Started on a SCUBA Photo Trip.** And then, each invited friends along on the adventure. Intertwined in the purpose of the book is the goal of helping you **"invite-a-friend."** The "fun factor" was multiplied by sharing the experiences with our friends.

"Invite-a-Friend" is a powerful concept. It's an opportunity to increase your enjoyment and spread the fun to your friends. The complexity comes about when you feel responsible for their enjoyment of the trip. The idea of this book is that if you follow the methods presented here – guiding you with the preparation for a live aboard underwater photo safari – the complexities become manageable. You will feel good about inviting your friend.

This book is a great assistant in preparation for your adventure. The discussions of pitfalls and the presentation of an almost complete checklist (it is never complete; however, the checklist in the appendix is the most fleshed out of any we have seen) will help you understand what is needed. Explanations of what actions must be accomplished and what items must be packed will increase your confidence that you are ready for the trip. This checklist is also broken down into time periods to ensure that you accomplish everything with plenty of time to spare and that the items on the checklist are purchased, checked-out, trained with, prepped for the trip, and packed properly. This series of recommended actions (by time prior to departure) and items to be included is presented in the appendix.

The four authors have been amateur photographers "of renown" for over 40 years with friends and family requesting copies of our best images. In addition, the group has extensive SCUBA diving experience (except for Chuck who doubled his dives – 25 to 50 – on this Peter Hughes trip) with one past dive instructor and dives in all the oceans (except the Arctic or Antarctic – we are dedicated, not crazy) and many of the seas around the world. They range from the Galapagos to Fiji, Indonesia, Papua New Guinea, the Great Barrier and Belize Reefs, Gulf of California, the Caribbean, the Adriatic, Atlantic, and many lakes and quarry's. SCUBA diving has been a wonderful hobby for a total of [42 + 50+ 40+ 8] 140 years. In addition, each of us has published in our field of expertise (rocket science) as well as our first Step Zero book [by Adams, Swan & Swan].

Step Zero: Getting Started on a SCUBA Photo Trip

Book Approach: Our approach is to provide structure to the preparation for a live aboard underwater photo safari. We discuss the various aspects of a live aboard trip such as common traits, reasonable expectations, and some lessons learned. We also use examples of "oops" moments to remind us that we all make mistakes. A major contribution of this book toward SCUBA diving is the inclusion of the extensive checklist in the appendix. In addition, an example is used in chapter 5, which lays out the Step Zero II Process to help prepare for an underwater photo safari: A trip onboard Paradise Dancer in Indonesia. The book chapter layout is:

Chapter Title

1. Introduction
2. Live Aboard Strengths "Valet Diving"
3. Maximum Enjoyment from Planning
4. A Live Aboard Adventure: A Novice's View
5. A Live Aboard Example: Second Sailing of the Paradise Dancer
6. Preparation for Photography
7. Planning for On Board Enjoyment
8. Next Steps
   Appendix – Checklist for Preparation

"Invite-a-Friend": The authors of this book believe that bringing a friend along enhances the adventure and ensures maximum enjoyment during the whole process. Pete and Cathy have been diving together and traveling to adventures for over 40 years. We are not sure who invites whom to which event; but, we doubly enjoy the experiences each time because we are together. Dennis has multiple dive buddies who accompany him when his wife, Gale, is unable to go. Chuck is a veteran traveler; but, was the invitee on this trip and felt strongly that preparation was key to a very enjoyable trip.

Managing Expectations: During the preliminary discussions for a trip with a friend you would like to invite along, a key phrase is: management of expectations. The following four items will guide you:

Compatibility – When making a choice of friends to invite, you must remember that you will be on stressful international trips in planes, trains, and hotel rooms. In addition, live aboards have small rooms and tight spaces. The invited friend will be very close for many days. A <u>common expectation</u> of experiences is important.

Time Together – Does your friend understand the <u>trip parameters</u>? A live aboard underwater photo safari requires time together for planning and traveling as well as the actual live aboard. Our team recommends showing up two days prior to the boat's departure to ensure your luggage and dive gear show up prior to the boat leaving (one day is risky). The trip home usually includes at least a day in travel; so, the total time together is anywhere from two to five days greater than the boat adventure's duration.

SCUBA Skills Match – As your invited friend becomes your <u>de-facto dive buddy</u>, ensure that you set your expectations as to skill level and adventurousness. Does your buddy want to dive five times a day or twice? Does your buddy jump at all land excursions? Does you friend have similar sleeping patterns? These are some of the thoughts that help to set expectations for the trip.

Live Aboard Characteristics – The great adventure of diving on a live aboard is that it really falls under the category of "**valet diving**." You never lift a tank as the crew loads and unloads from dive tenders. You have freshwater showers on the dive deck after each dive and your equipment is safely stored on the dive deck by the crew. This strength must be understood; but, it is <u>not a cruise ship</u>. Your trip partner must recognize that there is no shopping, very limited land excursions, and limitations on size of common area, 19 other divers share the dive deck and camera room, no emails, limited phone coverage, and extensive diving operations to the exclusion of other vacation activities. While on the SCUBA live aboard, there is no golf, tennis, exercise room, night life, or shopping. Your partner's expectations must match the reality of a live aboard to ensure a pleasant week with maximum enjoyment.

Setting Expectations

While sharing thoughts with a friend who might be invited along, you must ensure that they understand the following as a part of setting expectations:

Desire to SCUBA dive – The reality is that there is not that much to do on a live aboard that is not oriented around underwater photo safari activities. As a result, guests usually dive three to five times each day. The schedule usually spans from before breakfast to a night dive. The boat normally changes locations at least once during the day and travels longer distances during the night while you sleep. The bottom line is that if you love to SCUBA dive, you are in the right place. If you do not expect to be deeply involved in the diving, bring your own entertainment.

Love to Travel – this trait is essential for underwater photo safaris that are international in scope. If you do not love the adventure of traveling to new places with your friends, your expectations must at least include quiet acceptance of the capriciousness of travel. Traveling by air in today's world requires excellent preparation and extra patience. We have found that two extra days at the beginning of the trip is virtually mandatory as many factors influence the success of each part of your trip. Part of the preparation is multiple books, videos, and a computer.

A Boat is still a Boat – No matter how plush the circumstances, the restrictions of small boat life is real and must be psychologically prepared for. There is no escape from the small spaces, no getting off on a whim, and no last minute opportunities to rush to the store, theater, or restaurant. The pleasures of a live aboard are great if you have prepared for being on the boat for the duration of the trip (seven to ten days).

In this book we address two major questions from many viewponts. We will leverage our methodology, Step Zero, enabling successful future trips by the reader. The lessons learned (many humorous – but not at the time) will be presented with the focus being the appendix checklist.

(1)   What must you accomplish for a successful underwater photo safari?
(2)   What must your friend accomplish for a successful underwater photo safari?

Special Note – The Single Traveler: During the development of this book, the authors chose to concentrate on "Invite-a-Friend." This should not detract from the beauty and fun of taking one of these adventures as a single traveler. When you book as a single traveler, you will be "roomed" with a person of the same gender. Or, at a higher price, you may purchase a single room. It was mentioned, and strongly reinforced, during our Paradise Dancer trip, that live aboard underwater photo safaris are excellent

venues for single travelers, including women traveling alone. The characteristics of a live aboard tend to reinforce the idea of joining a small group on a trip which minimizes the all alone, single, traveler feeling. The beauty of this situation versus a land based resort, is that there are a small number of guests (usually no more than 20), and the environment is inherently safe.

The guests get to know each other well; sharing of fun is really easy; teaming up on the dive deck is simple; sharing is assumed after the diving as the activities almost all occur inside the community space; and, it is easy to make friends in small spaces with few people. As a result of these factors, going on an underwater photo safari live aboard is an excellent idea for a single traveler looking for adventure. You are no longer a single traveler, you have eighteen or so new close friends. In addition, it is more fun to share your dives with others.

Using a Checklist: The Step Zero process depends upon being ready for the adventure. This has lead to the development of an appendix to assist the reader in understanding the actions necessary prior to an underwater photo safari. In addition, the equipment check list is extensive and assists even the most careful preparer. The list covers the necessary items for traveler, vacationer, photographer, snorkeler, SCUBA diver, and especially, those who are going on a full live aboard underwater photo safari. The authors hope that the appendix enables the reader to feel confident when embarking on an underwater photo safari.

Chapter 2: Live-Aboard Strengths "Valet Diving"

Live Aboard Experiences

The excitement of an underwater photo safari on a live aboard is tremendous. Expectations are great for bountiful beauty, pristine locations, and great friendships. The amazing reality is that the expectations are usually exceeded. Our dive group, The Rocket Scientists, have coined a term to illustrate the comfortable approach to an underwater photo safari. We call it "Valet Diving," and the term implies that the customer is accommodated in all their needs to include tanks, BC's, weights, regulators and in the small tenders for the five dives available each day. In addition, the service on the boat is wonderful and the meals are superb. All you have to do is show up and enjoy the spoiling. Why do we go on these trips? To have experiences that are remarkable and enjoy a period of activity that has focus and distance from the day to day stresses of life. The following experiences of the authors are representative of live aboard adventures open to all SCUBA divers, or SCUBA diver want-to-be's.

1. Seven Days in the Galapagos: For scientists, and science appreciators, a trip to Darwin's laboratory of life is phenomenal. The diversity of life both above the sea and within the ocean made every dive exciting and full of discovery. The cold water, over abundance of life, and remote locations led to a better understanding of the realities of living in hostile environs. Swimming with large sharks on every dive made the total experience memorable. The Peter Hughes boat had two Ecuadorian naturalists who were remarkable in both their knowledge and diving skills. The ten days were filled with memorable experiences only achievable where the evolution of life is visible on a daily basis below the surface of the ocean. The trip of a lifetime for a science aficionado.

2. Paradise Dancer Ten Days: The Peter Hughes live aboard out of North Indonesia was spectacular. The special environment centered around the fact that the islands were all volcanic and some were still active. The rain forest edged from the island right to the waterline and the calm winds and easy weather made the environment calming. The lovely live aboard was especially roomy with a leisure attitude that encouraged active relaxation. There were many "quiet spaces" where you could find solitude while on a ship with 40 people. The fact that the crew outnumbered the passengers helped the comfortable feel and ease of living.

3. Ten Days Diving Papua New Guinea: The exhausting trip from our homes to the New Britain Island area is amazing in itself with the process producing travelers stressed to the maximum. Once in the Walindi area, the Peter Hughes expedition met all expectations with remarkable dives such as one on a WW II Japanese Zero in 30 feet of water. Each dive in the area was calculated to share with the visitors the remarkable creatures in the South Pacific. The pigmy seahorse was so small some authors were unable to see it, even when pointed out. However, using a small camera with macro lens enabled the team to both see and capture the picture in detail with vivid color comparison. This dive adventure was definitely a once in a lifetime thing!

COMMON TRAITS OF A SCUBA LIVE-ABOARD

The live aboard experience is one that excites, pleases and amazes the underwater photo safari adventurer. The strengths of a live aboard are diverse while the disadvantages are seemingly small to boat savvy divers [who do not easily get sea sick]. Some basic characteristics of a SCUBA diving live aboard are:

Phenomenal Adventure
One Time Set-up
Pristine Locations
Three Meals a Day
Good Friends
Rest and Lounge Area
Easy Access to Diving

Phenomenal Adventure – The opportunity for most of us to travel to exotic locales and partake in undersea adventures is limited to books and movies… until one signs up for an underwater photo safari on a live aboard. The ability to see Darwin's laboratory; the surprises available when exploring lightly charter waters in the Caribbean; and, the remote waters of Papua New Guinea all led the authors to adventures they still talk about. The search for a pygmy seahorse focused a whole group of divers for many days. The observation of large sharks in the waters around you definitely stimulated the adrenal glands. Indeed – adventure is the middle name of the underwater photo safari on a live aboard.

Pristine Locations – The ability of a ship to leave the populated parts of the world enables the live aboard guest to dive on sites not visited by "day boats." This capability to reach and investigate new and exciting dive locations make the live aboard experience special. On the Paradise Dancer in Northern Indonesia, the dives were all in areas of limited previous diving and in some cases completely new dive sites with the opportunity to name them.

> **Memorable Events – Live Aboard Galapagos Sharks**
>
> The marine biologists who accompany dive boats in the Galapagos ensure that everyone knows that local sharks have never attacked a diver. This is important as there are eight to ten foot sharks in your vision on each dive. The ultimate in my trip was at the farthest location from the airport, when we fell into the water suited up for cold water and hopefully an original adventure. And, it was! As I went down

> I cleared my mask and as the bubbles rose around me I saw 15 large sharks in front of me coming my way... 10 sharks on my left, 30 or so below me, and even some behind me who had already passed by without my noticing. As I knew there was a wall on my right about 20 feet away, I looked right for a quieter location.... Oops, about 5 sharks between me and the wall. The good news is they were fat sharks and not hungry. There is so much life in the waters around the Galapagos, the sharks grow large because there are many fish.... No need to take divers! I finished the dive with very rapid vision rotation; but, I only accomplished about 60% of the dive as my breathing was abnormally rapid – I wonder why?

Good Friends – As discussed earlier, the ability to invite a friend along is a privilege and should be enjoyed. The friends you travel with, and then dive with, are special and multiply your enjoyment and experiences. These friends are especially important as your expectations are to have fun, relax, and dive in locations you have never been to before. One remarkable strength, of live aboards, is the opportunity to develop strong friendships with new acquaintances as well. Common interests, similar expectations, and exciting challenges in remote locations lead to sharing of experiences and formation of natural friendship. Everyone on a ship ends up close to others as they dive, eat, and relax together. Sharing of experiences leads to budding friendships which lead to email exchanges and then future dive adventures.

One Time Setup: One significant strength of a dive live aboard is the process of diving. Each diver only has to set up their equipment one time at the start of the trip. After the first dive, the equipment returns to the same specific locations. The heavy lifting is accomplished by crew members, so literally, the diver never lifts a tank, or weight belt. The camera table is similar in that at the beginning of the week dive cameras are distributed around and essentially return to those spots. The rest of the week is easy as you return to the same table area to work on your underwater cameras. A key aspect of a boat, everything needs to be "ship shape," lends itself to convenience for divers.

Three Meals a Day: The beauty of living on a ship is that the chef is always there. The meals are usually structured around the dives while the diversity is sufficient to satisfy most travelers. After exercising in the ocean two/three/four or five times each day, the calories at meals are important. The diversity of the food on a live aboard is remarkable given they do not dock for days on end. The trips we have been on have all had excellent meals to include hearty breakfasts, lunches full of fruit, and dinners made with special local products. One problem has surfaced on every trip – the boats NEVER have enough oreo cookies!

Rest & Lounge Area: The day is scheduled for diving and the evening is laid out for entertainment. Five dives a day is a busy schedule – while preparation and post-processing of images consumes time. As a result, the rest and lounge areas are central locations where many gather to talk and compare notes on the diving and photography. In addition, the lounge is an excellent location for napping or reading a book. Movies are shown on most evenings.

Easy Access to Diving: The live aboard experience enables one to see how easy diving can be. The diver "suits up," attends a dive briefing on the dive deck, grabs fins, snorkel, mask and camera and then walks to the panga ladder. Once the divers are in the panga, they slip into the straps of the BC/tank/weights, and then fall into the water. After the dive, the process is reversed with the heavy lifting accomplished by the crew.

> ### Memorable Events – Bahamas Harry Potter Book
>
> As I bought the newest Harry Potter book on the first day of sales in the Miami airport at 0600, and immediately boarded an airplane to the Bahamas, and then directly onto the boat... no one else had an opportunity to buy the greatly sought after tome. Once we settled into the routine and I started reading the book, I would put it down in the lounge to go diving. Then I began to notice multiple pages turned down to mark other readers' progress. I found out that the Captain, cook and pursuer were all reading my book when it was placed on the table. They all came to me individually and pleaded that I not take this huge book with me and leave it for them to finish. On the last night, I had to stay up late to finish... or face the wrath of the crew.

The Spoiling Factor: During these live aboard adventures, the spoil factor is great. Once you are picked up from the hotel and have boarded the live aboard, the crew takes over and ensures you do not "want for anything." Your room is cozy, the meals are scheduled and special, freshwater is plentiful, drinks are available 24/7 [except that two of the authors ran two separate boats out of diet coke], diving is fantastic and the quiet is exquisite. Each diver believes the entire boat is focused upon their personal needs. It is amazing how divers can really focus on diving and relaxing when protected from the day-today chores of cooking, filling tanks, working and commuting. One example really exemplifies the activities of the supporting crews on the live aboard dive boats: the hot freshwater showers after every dive.

> **Memorable Events – Indonesia 82 Year Old Diver**
>
> One of the most experienced divers on our boat, was 82 years old and spry. He was exciting to be with as he discussed other dive sites and adventures. The key is that he had chosen "valet diving" as it was too difficult to lift and carry tanks and weights up and down cliffs or stairs. We are all hoping to be in his shape when we reach his diving experiences. Expectations must be realistic!

On the Peter Hughes boats, there is a custom that ensures each diver will be spoiled. As the diver comes up from the dive tender after a strenuous dive, the on deck hot freshwater showers greet them to rinse wetsuit and skins. After peeling off the apparatus, the exhausted diver stands under the hot freshwater shower for a few minutes to wash off the salt. After the shower, a crewman takes a hot towel and rubs down the shoulders for a good two minutes. Now that is spoilage!

Many other small things happen all week ensuring that every diver feels they are special. At 5 pm on the Paradise Dancer, a gin and tonic showed up for one diver [of course it was refused if a night dive was to be accomplished]. In addition, prior to each dive, cool water was provided to each diver in a glass on the dive deck to help battle de-hydration in the tropics. Indeed this set of authors has a new motto:

Valet Diving -- you dive, they tote!

TYPICAL DAY -- TYPICAL SCENARIO[1]

This is a "Sample Paradise Dancer – North Sulawesi Itinerary Only."

Saturday: Pickup at the Monado International Airport for transfer between the airport and Paradise Dancer. Boarding of Paradise Dancer begins in the afternoon. Each guest will check in with the hostess – this is primarily to validate certifications and levels of experience [bring your SCUBA

---

[1] directly from the Peter Hughes website covering the Paradise Dance in North Sulawasi, Indonesia:

cert cards]. Passengers are then escorted to their staterooms, dinner is provided onboard at approximately 6:30 pm, and an orientation slide show is presented after dinner.

Sunday to Saturday to Monday (8 Days): Most guests have the opportunity for up to five dives per day between the first morning dive and when the dive deck closes after the night dive. A dive bell is rung to signal the start of a dive briefing on the Main Deck. The vessel will usually dive two sites a day. Two morning dives are typically conducted at the first location of the day, after which the vessel is moved to a second location, for two afternoon dives and the night dive. Breakfast, lunch, dinner and after-dive snacks are provided each day. Dives sites usually include Lembeth Strait Bangka Islands, Bunaken National Marine Park, Siau and Sangihe Islands (depending upon weather conditions).

Tuesday: One early morning dive (starting at 6:00 am) and one right before lunch are scheduled before returning to port in the afternoon (usually between 3 and 5 pm). Breakfast and lunch are provided on board. Arrangements can be made from the vessel if guests wish to schedule a half-day inland tour when returning to port. An informal dinner is prepared on board at approximately 6:00 pm, or guests may elect to visit a local restaurant at their own expense.

Wednesday: Continental breakfast is available at 7:00 am. Disembarkation is at 8:00 am for all guests. Transfers to the airport are provided. Guests who are scheduled on a later flight may enjoy spending a few hours in town before returning to the airport.

The key to the live aboard experience is that it enables divers to concentrate on SCUBA diving. The traits have been explained through examples; and, hopefully, lead the reader to recognize that long travel times are well worth the excitement and challenges that you face and conquer. Indeed, they lead to a greater experience:

Valet Diving -- you dive, they tote!

CHAPTER 3: MAXIMUM ENJOYMENT FROM PLANNING

INTRODUCTION

Traveling the world on a once in a lifetime trip called an underwater photo safari is stimulating and tiring at the same time. The new vista's, cultures, and basic adventure ensures that the trip will be worthwhile and counted as one of your life's memorable events. You must look forward to all phases of the adventure to make sure the trip is phenomenal. To initiate this wonderful look at a new venture, one must start at the beginning believing that the whole process should be anticipated and then enjoyed during execution. As such, we always try to ensure that each of our dive buddies gains maximum enjoyment during the planning phases of the trip. It turns out that when you "Invite-a-Friend," you feel obligated to share the fun of the trip. A major part of enjoyment is the anticipation.

As a result, we have always considered the planning phase as one to be enjoyed and shared. Our group of dive buddies essentially communicate through emails; and then, we gather together to energize the spirit of adventure. These dive parties usually celebrate the recent trips of our members and prepare for the next. The last dive party was attended by the whole group and had three phases:

1 – Eat – drink – be merry

2 – Review past trip experiences to include passing out a series of DVD's with photos and slide shows; author's signing recent SCUBA book based upon previous group trips; gifts of photo album comprising last trip photos; and, showing the DVD slide show on a wide screen theater set up.

3 – General discussions on the next series of group dive trips – to include likely locations and appropriate dates. The fun of this dive party really heightens the enjoyment of previous trips and ensures that the anticipation levels start to rise for upcoming underwater photo safaris.

SCHEDULES & CHECKLISTS

The use of schedules is required to make sure the total team is "on-base" as to the progress of the adventure. While trying to ensure that the fun meter is pegged with enthusiasm during the anticipatory parts of the process – one must accomplish things in some semblance of order.

Days prior to Live Aboard

Action	Days Prior Boarding	Comments
Determine to Go	180	Need to Kick off your processes
Make Ship reservations	120	Many times the ship fills early
Medical & Work approval	120	Always a good move to get pills
Airline & Hotel reserve.	120	To ensure your reservations
Check-out & Buy equipment	50	Lay out all equipment
Test all Equipment	30	Testing in pool and fit-check
Flights to Location	3	Always allow 2 days prior to boat
Board Live Aboard	0	First day activities keep busy
Dive, Dive Dive	+ 10	Excitement
Flights Home	+ 12	Long trip home

Maximum Enjoyment from Planning • 17

This book's appendix is of invaluable assistance to the reader in understanding the actions necessary to prepare for an underwater photo safari. The first part is a set of actions that need to be reviewed and accomplished. The applicable actions for the reader's next trip should be obvious and fall out in a timely manner. In addition, the equipment check list is extensive and assists even the most careful preparer. The list covers items necessary for the traveler, vacationer, photographer, snorkeler, SCUBA diver, and, especially, the lucky ones who plan on a live aboard underwater photo safari. Not all items are necessary for each trip (nor for each individual on each trip); however, concerted effort should be made to coordinate equipment, backup items and repair tools amongst dive partners.

A set of four tables lays out critical actions that are necessary to successfully negotiate the planning processes. The Dave Letterman "top five list" approach was used to illustrate the strength of the appendix checklists. These steps can definitely be done for other than an underwater photo safari and the checklists have often been used for other trip types. Not all items must be accomplished by each trip participant; but, each item should be reviewed and, with forethought, marked completed or not marked after consideration.

	Title	*Special Feeling*	*Time Prior to Departure*
L	Long-Term	Anticipation Starts	9-12 mo's
M	Mid-Term	Excitement Builds	4-8 mo's
S	Short-Term	Excitement Almost Real	1-3 mo's
LC	Last Chance	Almost There	Weeks prior

Trip planning starts with the decision to go on a live aboard for an underwater photo safari adventure. Once that decision has been made, the winnowing down options begins. The group gets together and discusses the various opportunities and what potential difficulties may arise for members who may want to go. After a lot of discussion, a preliminary decision is made and the whole team starts their individual planning to get to the chosen location. The concept that works best in our dive group is:

Group Consensus – Individual Actions

The most experienced person in the preliminarily chosen geographic area is usually on point for chasing down the options on destination targets, airline options, land options, advantages, disadvantages, and any other items that they can find. Usually after a month or two, the adventure is defined by which boat [we chose Paradise Dancer in North Indonesia for our example], which airline [we chose Singapore Airline for its Star alliance relationship and free mileage availability], how many days prior to the yacht departure [we chose at least 2 days for each of us near Manado], and where to stay overnight if it's not possible to make it in one continuous trip [we chose Singapore]. One of the concepts that we like is the addition of a short island vacation prior to boarding the ship. Most of the planning can be accomplished using the internet and the wonderful information available about all the live aboards and locations around their departure locations. One key item of concern is the airline price variation, so a continuous searching for "deals" leads to the best prices which vary so much over seasons and airlines. After the discovery process is over, the emails between dive buddies enable each to be kept up to speed on the activities. The checklist at the end of the book has the full list of items that must be assessed and accomplished – both actions and equipment to purchase and pack.

L	Long-Term Anticipation Starts
Top 5	Recommended Actions
	9-12 Months
1	Preliminary Itinerary – Where & When to go?
2	Plan on vacation from work
3	Make dive resort reservations
4	Check passport expiration
5	Schedule Planning parties

This is the time that usually leads to best price selections for airlines and hotels, so go ahead and make reservations. If you are too worried about the ability to make the trip for reasons such as health or some other emergency, trip insurance is an option. This "excitement builds" time period is also best for vaccinations to ensure there are not allergic reactions or shortages of medicine. However, the best usage of this time is to spend it with your equipment and start building excitement. Regulators, flash units, emergency beacon lights, masks and other equipment should be pulled out of storage, washed off and experimented with. Camera gear tends to not like long layoffs and SCUBA equipment tends to stagnate if not cleaned sufficiently and stored correctly. As a result, early inspection is worthwhile on these items. One item that is not always thought of is the compatibility of your equipment and clothing with your international weight restrictions and baggage sizes. Read the instructions from the airline and the live aboard and ensure that your baggage capability matches the requirements of the guys in-charge. Also, the timeline for passports and visas are such that you cannot wait until the last minute and reasonably expect to have the government react to your emergency. Checkout your passport and visa requirements early and do whatever is necessary to get this accomplished.

M	Mid-Term Excitement Builds
Top 5	Recommended Actions
	4-8 months
1	Get appropriate shots/vaccinations
2	Service SCUBA equipment (regulator etc)
3	Buy new equipment – SCUBA and camera
4	Pool test everything
5	Purchase DAN SCUBA insurance

The ten day (or seven day) live aboard experience can be maximized with proper planning – which includes the ability to enjoy the various diving possibilities. If it has been a long time since the last dive, practice in a pool is highly recommended. If you would like to use Nitrox [enhanced Oxygen usage for fewer headaches and longer stays underwater – at the cost of max depth], then certification is necessary well ahead of the trip. A quick review of the diving protocols [like safety stops, dive computer usage, and hand signals] should be accomplished and practiced by you and your buddy.

S	Short-Term Excitement Almost Real
Top 5	*Recommended Actions*
	1-3 months
1	Complete your consolidation of travel stuff
2	Ensure enough prescription drugs for trip
3	Reconfirm all reservations
4	Assemble all equipment and test
5	Mark all equipment with name

This "last chance" phase of planning is right before the execution phase; but, it is really important. Some things people forget are to check the weather around your location and the "where am I going to stash the kids, cat, or dog" questions must be answered. It turns out that the good planner has very little to do at this time besides practice packing. The one who waits until the last minute will end up with things that are almost impossible to achieve without herculean efforts on their part and others [who sometimes do not cooperate]. We feel as though the planning process should be part of the full enjoyment of the trip. You anticipate the actual activities while you are making reservations or practicing the use of a dive computer.

LC	Last Chance – Almost There
Top 5	***Recommended Actions***
	Weeks prior
1	Pack dive certification cards
2	Pack passports
3	Get final medicines and "comfort items"
4	Tell neighbors you are going
5	Throw 10 pounds out of your luggage

Critical planning activities are listed in the four sidebar charts and reflect the checklist items in the appendix. However, nothing is written in stone. Variability is great on when to do each step or in what order. We have written them down in time periods which we believe leads to the smoothest transitions to successful trips. We all know that if you were to be invited on the most wonderful trip which leaves tomorrow – and really does not significantly impact your current life – you would choose "of course" and panic to get everything accomplished that needed to be done. However, the risk and the cost are definitely increased on these sudden trips. If you remember the days when you were young, single and on your own – it was often – "Lets go!" The key is that the checklist of actions to accomplish and equipment to bring shown in the appendix, is a suggested set of guidelines that will lead to fewer hassles and work-arounds during your live aboard adventure. It seems to us that this 12 month "enjoy the anticipation" process can easily be gone through in six months, or even two months; but, where is the fun in that? One very important item in the weeks prior timeline is medicine and pills. One friend had a great time with that one – see memorable event (Manado Customs).

TRAVEL HEALTH

One important aspect of a SCUBA travel vacation is tending to your travel health. Unlike equipment, most of the issues with health are private and not discussed with others. The topic is presented here and in the checklist which provide excellent recommendations of medical items to carry with you.

In the **pre-trip** period you must have your health assessed by a medical professional. SCUBA diving is a physical sport that can be life endangering if you are not physically ready. Even those who may have physical disabilities may SCUBA dive if they have had a medical evaluation. When you take the proper precautions and know your limitations, you too can enjoy the wonders of the world beneath the sea.

> ### Memorable Events – Manodo customs
>
> Upon arriving at the Manado airport from Singapore on Silk Air, Barry, Jerry and Dennis departed the plane to get a "visa on arrival" and to claim their bags. All went well. They got their visas quickly. With their bags in tow, they started to proceed through Customs where they figured they would not have a problem. Dennis was waived right through with Barry and Jerry right behind. Dennis went out the glass door, looked for the hotel bus (didn't expect one but was looking just in case), found a nice quite place to stand so the group could talk and discuss how to get to the hotel. At this point, Dennis looked back, and to his surprise, Barry and Jerry were gone!! After 90 curious minutes the incident was resolved. The customs inspector, who had waived Dennis right through, had stopped Barry and Jerry just as they were to exit the door and Dennis didn't notice. The inspector made them go back to the inspection area and went through their bags where he found unmarked pills in plastic bags. The pills were a 30 day supply of generic vitamins that each had brought but had discarded the packaging to save space. After much discussion, having the pills chemically tested and paying a $1.00 USD fine, they were permitted to exit the arrival area to join Dennis.
>
> Moral of the story,
> a. follow the advice in the book
> b. carry all medications on your person for easy inspection and loss prevention
> c. keep all markings on the items, over-the-counter, or prescription
> d. keep an extra copy of your prescriptions with you should you need to refill lost item
>
> Yep, this little incident may have been avoided had Barry and Jerry followed the steps listed in the checklist. Keep medicines in original packages!

It is in this pre-trip period when we become physically fit and obtain our medications. The checklist will guide you with assembling your kit. The basic concept is that you will be in a remote area and not near your favorite home pharmacy – you need to take medical items to treat minor injuries or conditions. A small bag of little items in your room will ensure your privacy and your ability to use them when you need them. Hotels or boats will be able to assist you with major issues; but, there is nothing like having your own kit in your room. An excellent internet site for exploring medical conditions and SCUBA diving is www.SCUBA-doc.com. But remember, there is no substitute for a checkup by your personal physician.

The more difficult period of your travel health is when you are **on your trip**. You will be encountering medical environments that your body is not familiar with and are out of your control. If there is one piece of advice you should heed, it is to STAY CLEAN. There is no better protection. The airplane trip is the **first** hazardous environment you will encounter. There are sick people on the plane coughing and sneezing and touching everything. If you are close to someone who is ill, move if you can. If you cannot change seats (very hard to do on today's crowded flights) then stay clean. Washing your hands or using a hands cleanser is the single best thing you can do on your trip. You will encounter health hazards during the remaining portion of your trip but none as focused as on an airplane.

The **second** most hazardous item is your personal action. I follow these guidelines and they seem to work for me.

1. Drink plenty of bottled water – wash hands
2. Eat foods that are well cooked or breads that are fresh – wash hands
3. Use insect repellant – wash hands
4. Use sun screen – wash hands
5. Stay clean – wash hands.

The rest is common sense. A humorous phrase we use is "don't drink it unless it goes "Pheeeft" when you open it and don't eat it unless it is burnt." Many people will try and drink only alcohol but your body needs water. Good clean water prevents a lot of ills and if you are SCUBA diving you need to offset the dry air from the tank. Do not get dehydrated.

When you SCUBA dive you will need to follow a few simple rules.

1. Protect your skin – wear a wet suit
2. Protect your skin – use sunscreen
3. Protect your ears – use an ear wash after your dive
4. Protect your insides – don't drink the ocean water

The wet suit not only keeps you warm, but will keep the sun off your body as you are moved on the dive tender or shore boat to the dive site. Stay out of the sun. The sun in the tropics is very strong; and, if you do not take precautions, your skin will burn in a very short period of time. Sunscreen protects the parts of your body the wetsuit does not cover. Your face is always exposed, so coat it liberally. Some of the new brands also claim to have insect repellant; also, coat the back of your hands. They will be sitting in your lap or hanging on a safety rail. Your ears will gather water as you dive and mostly drain when you reach the surface. The water in the ocean contains living things, both good and bad. One common prevention measure is to use an ear wash after every dive. These simple guidelines will save you many problems. Do not let the above frighten you. Just take the appropriate health measures. You look both ways prior to crossing the street so you are already trained to take care of yourself. You just need to follow the appropriate steps for having a safe and enjoyable SCUBA trip. Others do – so can you. An excellent article on SCUBA health and infections was in Undercurrent (Vol. 22, No. 2, Feb 2007).

Secure Electronic Storage for Lost Documents

"What do I do if I lose my identity documents?" Don't worry; chances are you won't lose them. But, if you do, there are simple steps that can get you back rapidly into the swing of things. The travel documents you should consider protecting via this process are: passports, visas, credit cards with international 800 or collect call contact numbers, E-Tickets, reservation confirmations, travel location and resort phone numbers, home and friend phone numbers, and email addresses. Prior to leaving home, make multiple copies of your travel documents and keep them in separate areas of your belongings. For example, keep the originals in your personal "carry-with-you-everywhere" bag. This bag should be small, bland looking and easy to carry with a strong strap you can wrap around yourself. You may want to consider putting some of your documents into a "keep-inside-your-clothing" pouch so the pouch and documents will be out of easy viewing. These work very well for things you don't need easy access to such as your backup credit cards and cash. One thing to remember is that in hot climates you will perspire. This may be mitigated by putting the items in a small plastic bag. You should then store copies of your needed travel documents in various places of your luggage or swap copies with your fellow traveler. This way if your prime documents end up missing, you will have copies to get you on your way until you restore your prime documents. For most ordinary events, such as hotel confirmation numbers and airline E-tickets, copies will work just fine.

Passports and Visas must be original if they are to be accepted by immigration, customs, police and airline officials. Keep copies of these documents separated from the originals. The likelihood of losing them both is small. However, if you lose your original passport, getting a replacement should be your first priority. When you are in a foreign land, without a passport, you are a person without a county. But, if you have a copy of your passport, you are on your way back to normalcy. If you recorded the phone number, location and time of service of an Embassy as stated in the "Action" section of this book, all you have to do is call the embassy and request assistance in getting a replacement passport. This usually takes one working day. If you are in the backwater of some remote location and a long way from an embassy, then the paper copies of your documents will usually suffice with the local officials who will assist you in getting to your embassy. If you severely damage your passport, such as leaving it in a pants pocket when they are run though the laundry, do NOT attempt to repair the passport yourself. Anything you do to the passport may look like you are trying to modify it. Just take whatever comes out of the laundry and protect it in a plastic bag. And keep a copy of the good passport with it. The page with your photo and other information is plastic coated will probably survive well enough to get you back into the "documented persons" status. (On a personal note, I have seen 4 passports go though the laundry and they worked well enough to get the people back home) One person had extra time and went to the embassy while she was overseas. Yes, she got a lecture on how to safeguard the passport. But because she had a copy of her original passport, it was very easy for the embassy to verify her status and issue a replacement.

An emerging concept and supporting technology is to keep copies of your documents in the "secure internet cloud." You can lose all paper originals and backup copies to the bottom of the ocean or a hotel fire and still get back in business. This is possible through the magic of the internet. If your documents are totally lost, all you need to do is to find a computer with internet access, log into your account and download or print the documents or data you need from those items you scanned and uploaded to this storage site prior to your trip. You can then take these copies of your lost documents and proceed with the restoration process or use the data to press on with your trip. Now for the technical part, how should you store your documents on the internet? Security is the prime issue. For documents and data that are not too private, such has hotel reservations, phone numbers of those at home and e-tickets, you may want to bundle them into a folder and e-mail them to yourself. Then all you must do is log onto your email service and print what you need. For documents that are more sensitive such as credit card numbers and the associated 1-800 numbers to call for help you will want a more secure means of storage. (also you may want to store passwords, pins or the 3 digit code on the back) There are several free encryption programs that will serve your needs well. True Crypt or AxCrypt encryption utilities and the Apple Mobile Me, Carbonite, and other on-line storage and backup systems are but a few of the alternatives. More are coming on line every day and many are free if you endure a little advertising. You don't need much on-line secure storage. You only have a few documents. This added protection does not come without some negatives. You will need to remember more passwords to decrypt the data in these programs and may need special software to be added to your emergency computer. These are small issues that may be easily resolved given the emergency conditions you may find yourself in. When you do get your sensitive documents such as copies of your passports, credit cards numbers (including the three digit code on the back), along with the emergency overseas call collect for help number, the security risk of downloading this data to a strange computer and of printing the data on a strange server and printer is small compared to the advantage you have gained. You are now able to buy things with your credit card information and call your emergency numbers. You may need this data.

You should not leave this data on the computer you have just borrowed. There is a very small chance someone will discover it even if you don't save it on this strange computer – but what choices do you have. You are in a bad, non-status, situation and all you want is out. Do what you have to do. Destroy the computer records on the strange computer as best as you can. Recover later when you are home. You need your credit card company phone numbers so you can call them, cancel your old cards and get new cards.

These few steps are easy to accomplish in your trip preparation phase and will provide you with the peace of mind that if you lose all your documents, all is not lost. Welcome to the association of Global Travel, perils and all. Others travel to exotic and remote places, so can you. Just do it.

Post Trip Products: One important item in the planning process should have special notice in this book. We call it preparing for the post trip products. Remember the family album of films or still photos from those family trips. Indeed they have importance for the ones that take the pictures and enjoy the trips; but, they have even more importance for those who were not there but are part of the extended family. As an example, I just received some photos of my grandparents' trip to China in the early part of the 20th century. It was a pleasant surprise to receive a little family history and touch my grandparents across the years. The question should start with... "What do I want to have after the trip?" Some answers are:

- A series of post cards
- A series of stamps from each location
- A set of thimbles from each location
- A different set of playing cards representing various experiences
- A bound album of photos
- A CD or DvD of pictures
- A video of the trip
- A combination of many of the above

A key to ensuring that you will have "post trip products" is early planning concerning the various factors. Bringing the appropriate parts for each set of equipment becomes important. For an underwater photo safari on a live aboard, the supply store is not accessible. As a result, if you want something to happen you must have that part – and a back up or a repair capability (see chapter on photographic preparation). Once again the dive group and dive buddies should discuss the options for post trip products. Our group ensures that all have digital photo capability and plan for backup parts to be carried. Usually, our buddies travel with their digital cameras (land and underwater), the equipment to down load from the cameras, a laptop (each has preferences for PC or Mac), and usually enough DvD's to backup the trip experiences (and to share with our new friends).

Chapter 4: A Live-Aboard Adventure: A Novice's View

Introduction

The underwater photo safari experience is a challenge from many angles, not the least of which is the intimidation factor –

What am I getting myself into?

This chapter is written by one of the authors who was a novice diver who had never been on an international SCUBA trip to a live aboard. The uninitiated will look at the offer from friends and wonder –

Why should I do this?
How tough is it?
How far is Indonesia?
How can this possibly work?
How can I explain to my significant other?
How can I possibility pull this off?

This chapter addresses the puzzling time when you are trying to accept or turn down an invitation to join a friend.

Trip Preparation

After deciding that yes, I could be happy spending a week and a half trapped on a dive boat with my friend – I started getting ready for the trip. I had never been on a dive this far from home and was a bit concerned about how to prepare. Luckily, my friend had just published a book, **Step Zero: Getting Started on a SCUBA Photo Trip**. While not written expressly for a live-aboard situation, it contained enough information on getting ready for photographic diving that I was well prepared. I especially leveraged the checklists and suggestions. The checklists covered most of the dive and photo gear items I would need. The book also addressed ways to safely pack the checked and carry-on luggage. And yes, my checked luggage was opened and inspected somewhere enroute; and, yes, the hasp for one of the locks was broken leaving my checked luggage unlocked forever-more.

Luckily for me (because I read the book) I had packed my expensive cameras, lenses and other electronic gear in my carry-on luggage. It was heavy, but I did not risk losing all my expensive gear. It also provided the benefit of allowing me to play with my toys on the 16 hour flight.

Preparation for the trip was one of those experiences where assistance was greatly appreciated. The first thing to do is, of course, discuss and decide with your spouse or close friends the major item – I am going, alone or with you? The next two items in time sequence are – Can I get off work; and I better make airline reservations. My dive buddy helped me accomplish the items on the checklist in a timely manner with the recognition of time criticality: what must be done first and by when? The checklist in the back of this book is the best that we can develop to show timelines for actions and what must be brought along.

Memorable Events – Self Query?

All that money? All that time? All that work to prepare? But, what an adventure it could be! So many things to think about... I have never been on a boat (or is it a ship?) for 10 days, much less a rather small one with 20 other people. Do I really want to do this?

> Here's the deal: My friend Pete had asked me if I wanted to join him and Dennis, his dive buddy for 40 years, on a dive trip half-way around the world. It would be on the Paradise Dancer, a beautiful three-masted schooner based in Indonesia. What should I do? How well do I really know Pete and who is this Dennis guy anyway? Will I have a memorable adventure or a miserable trip? Do I understand all that is expected of me? Am I prepared for such a long dive trip so far from home ?
>
> Oh what the heck, it's an adventure. Let's go!

After planning and packing, the trip commenced with some level of trepidation. As such, having friends helping you accomplish everything up to that point makes it an acceptable level of concern. In fact, confidence at the front door as you leave for your underwater photo safari is the desirable outcome of excellent planning and extensive use of the checklists. Our trip to Indonesia was indeed booked with respect to events like missed flights or broken airplanes and lost luggage. However, the excitement was felt by all and especially enjoyed as expectations were high for a marvelous trip of a lifetime. A stop-over in Singapore, a Singapore Sling at Raffles, a quick flight over Borneo, and all of a sudden the plans and checklist actions had all been executed successfully. Amazing!

Pre-ship Delight: We had the extra benefit of a five day stay at the Gangga Island Resort and Spa. Aside from the fact that this place was "heaven on earth," it afforded us a chance to get in some practice diving prior to the Paradise Dancer experience. As they say on their web-site, "for both divers and non-divers the picturesque white sand beach, the large salt-water pool, a traditional spa and the high quality of service at Gangga Island Resort will guarantee a peaceful and relaxing stay."[2] We ate great food, slept in little cabins steps from the waves and hiked around playing with our cameras. We did dive every day and followed it up with

---
[2] From http://www.ganggaisland.com/

a daily massage. Well, someone had to do it! After my first dive, I surfaced and spotted a fisherman a few feet away. This captured the real emotion of being a million miles away from home. This was really extra credit diving and by the end of that five days I was ready for the next phase - On to the Ship – Paradise Dancer.

On The Ship: After all my preparations I finally arrived on the ship and was under control, pretty much... I had my passport, SCUBA gear and my underwater camera gear ready to go. I was given a bunk, shown around and felt ready to start diving. Or so I thought.

> ### Memorable Events – When is a Spare a Spare?
>
> When is a spare a spare? In dutiful preparation, I packed my primary and spare dive gear along with my wife's snorkeling gear and headed out. My first mistake in planning was counting my wife's primary mask as my backup mask -- my error was apparent as I watched her snorkeling as I left her at the Resort while I headed for the live-aboard. Half-way through the week, sure enough, I dropped my mask into the deep blue. Fortunately, Paradise Dancer anticipated my plight and had a "spare mask" for sale. My error was not anticipating the primary owner (wife) actually wanting to use her gear. A better sparing plan would have been three (or four) masks since there were two users, a cheap price to pay for a round-the-world dive trip. The ship bought mask was OK, but I would have had a better fit if I had brought along my own (not my wife's) backup mask.

Gear checkout - I had brought the recommended dive gear, including wetsuit, mask, fins, snorkel, BCD and dive computer (what a great invention!) and used the ship's air tank, regulator, and weights. All was going well for each dive as the ship believed in "valet diving" – meaning they do all the heavy lifting. On the third day, with great confidence, I boarded the dive launch where our BCD, weights and air tank were already loaded and waiting for us. What a way to go! When the dive was over we surfaced and floated the BCD, weights and air tank over to the side of the launch and helpful attendants lifted all that mass on board. Then, they served us cool 'drinks and drove us back to the live-aboard to eat and be merry. However, this pampering lulled me into a false sense of security that taught me a basic lesson in SCUBA. It's your equipment, it's your life – check everything twice; and, then do it again.

> ### Memorable Moments – Empty Tank Lesson
>
> When do I check out my gear? As the launch boat approached the dive spot, I noticed my air tank had accidentally not been refilled – it was empty! As the rest of the divers jumped in, I returned to the ship for a new air tank, then back to the dive spot and promptly dropped my original mask into the deep blue sea - gone. I returned again to the ship to borrow a mask and finally joined the rest of the divers. Incidentally, I found Pete's bright yellow snorkel at the bottom on the ocean where he had just dropped it. Even the best can lose something. Avoid the panic and drama and check the gear long before the launch starts moving. I did from then on.

Food - Pills, Prescriptions and Shots - I had them all. I had followed instructions to the "t," visited my doctor and was completely prepared for any medical contingency. Or so I thought. I pride myself on the ability to visit any and all hole-in-the-wall fine food establishments and not just survive, but thrive. Sometimes, the best food is found in the least expected places. Words to the wise: Pay attention to what you are eating and never think you are invulnerable.

Compatibility - I have known my dive buddy for about 15 years. He and his wife came to my wedding and we have spent time at each other's homes for visits and holidays. Our wives have been friends since they were toddlers. But was he someone I could share a small space with for ten days straight? Did we have compatible personalities or would the thin veneer of sociability wear off and the real jerk (his or mine) emerge? What about his dive buddy, and the rest of the dive members, such as my yet-to-be-experienced roommate?

> ### Memorable Events – Global Bugs
>
> The dinner tasted great, but by midnight I was very unhappy. Expect to have some stomach or head affliction (or both) when you meet and greet all of the new "bugs" living half way around the world. I had all of the necessary prescription drugs needed. I had all my shots and preventative pills, but neglected to seriously consider anti-diarrhea or laxatives as I had a "cast iron" stomach back home. So, I was surprised when a gurgling sensation down there put me down for 24 hours the 5th day of our voyage. The "bugs" back home are really pikers compared to the ones you have never met before. Fortunately, the Paradise Dancer anticipated my particular stomach affliction and was prepared to treat me.

My roommate turned out to be a great guy from Tennessee - accent and wit included. I was very fortunate to find that we had similar dive preferences and habits. He wanted to dive early and a few times a day (rather than 5) and that was perfect for me. We spent the afternoons working on our computers with the thousands of photos we took. We sorted, Photoshopped, and prepared slide shows to inflict upon our loved ones once we were home. Yes, I guess we are both nerdy rocket scientists. My dive buddy preferred to dive at a shallow depth to concentrate on ambient light for photography and so did I. Ambient light at shallow depths allowed our photos to look more natural. We both use our gas (air) at virtually the same rate so we surfaced at the same time. We enjoyed an adult beverage in the afternoons and knew enough to not dive afterwards. All in all, we got along famously.

The other members of the dive live aboard were equally interesting and fun. The Paradise Dancer is not huge but there was always a place to mix (or not) as the mood struck. We could retreat to our state rooms for quiet reading, socialize in the main salon with the dive group, or find a small place above deck to enjoy the incredible ocean and passing islands. Indeed, the limited environment of a live aboard lent itself to getting to know the other divers. These friends of friends and new acquaintances became new friends as the week went along. These new friends are sure to show up on future underwater photo safaris. I look forward to the next big adventure.

Chapter 5: A Live-Aboard Example: Second Sailing of the Paradise Dancer

Preparation for the Trip

Each of us on this wondrous live aboard underwater photo safari prepared using our checklist in the back of this book. As we have shown in the previous chapters, there are many activities that are essential to confidence as you leave on your trip. Here is a quick summary of how we took the checklist in the back and proceeded for this trip in the summer of 2008.

Long-Term Anticipation: It turns out that the most important aspect of our dive group is that we actively support each other both before and after we go on an adventure.

L	*Long-Term Anticipation Starts*	*9-12 Months*
Top 5	*Recommended Actions*	*Actions Taken*
1	Preliminary Itinerary – Where & When to go?	Oct 07 – North Indonesia
2	Plan on vacation from work	Check
3	Make dive resort reservations	Chose second cruise on purpose
4	Check passport expiration	8 + years left on each of ours
5	Schedule planning parties	3 parties prior to departure

Mid-Term Excitement Builds: This time period is more of an individual execution of group consensus. The training and the planning is definitely across the total spectrum of preparation and must be accounted for in some manner. We found that keeping the checklist up to date worked well at ensuring that actions are taken when necessary. We especially enjoyed buying point and shoot (P&S) underwater cameras as backup equipment.

M	*Mid-Term Excitement Builds*	*4-8 Months*
Top 5	*Recommended Actions*	*Actions Taken*
1	Get appropriate shots/vaccinations	Maleria pills and Typhoid shots
2	Service SCUBA equipment (regulator etc)	Tune up five months prior
3	Buy new equipment – SCUBA and camera	"Needed" new P&S camera
4	Pool test everything	P&S tested in saltwater pool
5	Purchase DAN SCUBA insurance	Definitely

Short-Term Excitement Almost Real: This preparation period is extremely important because you are now getting into the region where major issues will cause you to panic or miss the vacation. This is not the time to find out that your boss can not let you go during that time period.

S	*Short-Term Excitement Almost Real*	*1-3 Months*
Top 5	*Recommended Actions*	
1	Complete your consolidation of travel stuff	United changed flights, had to adjust
2	Ensure enough prescription drugs for trip	One month supply sufficient
3	Reconfirm all reservations	Hotels worked fine
4	Assemble all equipment and test	Strobes hooked into camera
5	Mark all equipment with name	White electrical tape works best

Last Chance – Almost There: The planning during this time period should have been laid our prior to this point. The only actions to really be accomplished at this juncture in time are the ones that needed to be last or "just in time." The fun one is the packing and the process of ensuring the weight limits are not inadvertently exceeded.

LC	Last Chance - Almost There	Weeks Prior
Top 5	Recommended Actions	
1	Pack dive certification cards	Made spare copy and put in a separate bag
2	Pack passports	Made spare copy & put in a separate bag
3	Get final medicines and "comfort items"	Talked with doctor about any changes
4	Tell neighbors you are going	Arranged for mail and paper pickup
5	Throw 10 pounds out	Measured weight very carefully

PRE-SAILING ACTIVITIES

The time period that exists between your departure from home, and the boat leaving the dock, should be planned for and enjoyed. This particular trip had each group going in different directions. Four of us went to Gangga Island, just outside of Manado (capital of North Sulawesi) airport. This enabled us to have fun and enjoy the island life style for five days prior to boarding the boat. Some of the members of this live aboard adventure actually stayed in Manado for three days and explored this land. Each of these approaches satisfied the need for "spare time" prior to departure from dock [nominally two days for SCUBA equipment and bags to catch up].

Gangga Island: For the group that went to the Gangga Island Resort, it was remarkable. The casual living at the resort matched the superb snorkeling and diving experiences. The cottages were excellent for divers (plenty of room – air conditioned – large showers – comfortable beds – TV, if you turned it on, with CNN and HBO). They also have a very large saltwater swimming pool to loll beside, as well as in. The four and five course meals were well presented with a wide range of choices and spices. Three meals were served in a spacious open air dining room. They also had a nice sitting area for cocktails and conversations. This area also contained a pool table and a multi-language book exchange style library.

Gangga Diving: The snorkeling was as good as anyplace we have been to include the Great Barrier and Belize reefs. The sea state was remarkably smooth without a ripple so that the transportation to and from the island and dive sites was like motoring in a bathtub. The crystal clear blue of the water was spectacular with shades indicating deep water to shallow with sand below. Morning and afternoon snorkeling are part of the resort services and deliver you to beautiful shallows (4 – 25 feet). While floating along in wonderland, a yell broke out and we all raised our heads to see a school of two dozen or so dolphins playing not far from us. We were in awe as they stayed near us and showed off. They would do the normal leaps and slaps of the water seemingly challenging each other to do better. So it started! Each did a little more... faster, higher, more amazing. Then two champions performed. One did a high speed forward leap and must have rotated around his axis three times (1080 degrees). The second guy decided to jump and do a flip... not forward, but backward. We all floated there for 20 minutes watching the show and were amazed! In addition, we swam with turtles and observed a plethora of small and colorful reef fish swimming around and through the marvelous coral and sea anemones, as well as an occasional ray. The diving was very pleasant with calm seas and phenomenal diversity in creatures. While diving at our four dive sites (Busa Bora Baret, Rainbow, and Secret Point on P. Bangka Island; Yellow Coconut on North Sulalizi), we were able to see large cuttle fish, blow fish, scorpion fish, red & black lion fish, large shrimp, ghost pipe fish, and my favorite, clown fish (black, brown, yellow, orange & grey) defending their homes.

Gangga Staff: The resort staff was superior with expertise and pleasant approaches. They clearly have a focus on customer satisfaction and quality of service. The twice daily cleaning of the room matched the morning and afternoon dive schedule. The meal staff ensured pleasant experiences with quick responses and recognition of you as their only concern. The dive staff enabled us to snorkel and dive as if it were our own special world – and it was! They dove with us and pointed out incredible sights we would have missed. The professional and happy staff at the spa made each visit more memorable than the last. Can you imagine a "hard day" at diving ending with a massage and then dinner and drinks (lots of ice tea was consumed).

Gangga Photography: For the photographer, both underwater and above water, the scenery is enticing. The clouds, rain storms, sunsets, and resort settings stimulated many "artistic" shots based upon colors and shadows while the variety of underwater creatures "tweaked" this camera bug into taking over 400 pictures in four dives. After my first dive, I surfaced and spotted a fisherman a few feet away. This image captured the real emotion of being a million miles away from home. This was really extra credit diving.

The Checklist for Gangga Island: It was fortunate that we used the checklist in the appendix preparing for the trip to Gangga and Paradise Dancer. The group had all the necessary equipment components for a successful underwater photo safari without any access to SCUBA stores or equipment replacements. The land resort prior to the live aboard enabled us to prepare for the adventure to follow. Indeed, the days prior to a live aboard can be productive as well as a safety value to ensure all equipment arrives with you at the live aboard dock.

<u>**Second Sailing of the Paradise Dancer:**</u> The new Peter Hughes' boat, Paradise Dancer, was sailing on its second passenger run north of Sulawesi when we joined in on the trip [North Sulawesi Islands May 24 – June 4, 2008]. The excitement was evident from the first contact at the airport through the hour ride to the Paradise Dancer. Everyone was looking forward to the "second sailing" of the new Peter Hughes dive boat. Not only was it to be the ultimate live aboard, but it placed each of us into an environment especially designed for an underwater photo safari. The ability to offer new sites and ones that have been only lightly dived enabled the Peter Hughes team to create anticipation among the guests. Each of us wanted to "hurry up" and get to this creatively designed three-masted schooner designed specifically for SCUBA diving in the Coral Triangle [area from the Solomons to Indonesia to the Philippines]. The concept that all of us signed up for was "valet diving" and it lived up

to it's advertising. The boat was remarkable, the dive spots were new and some even in the process of being discovered while the 19 person crew excelled at personal service.

The Boat: The boat lived up to the pre-sail hype in that the accommodations were luxurious and the ship was pleasing to the eye. The 50 meter long, 15 meters wide, motor yacht with nine sails was designed to resemble the sleek fast American schooners that sailed across the world from Boston and New York. Sleek lines and sailing excellence established the logical lines of design for those 19th century ships. These keys were then used as a baseline for the underwater photo safari luxury live aboard – the Paradise Dancer. She was built on an island in Borneo selected for its available huge hardwood beams. The wooden decks and hardwood cabinets ensured that the look was authentic, remarkable, and beyond even our elevated expectations. Each of the cabins seemed 50 % larger than previous live aboards with a bathroom you could spend time in. The shower was 3 x 4 feet and allowed room to move around – a serious pleasure after a long day soaking in the salt of the sea. The beds were roomy with a desk and plenty of storage space for each passenger. The boat was so silent that the night cruises between dive locations lulled one to sleep with no problem getting a full nights rest. The arrangements were such that you could actually spend plenty of time in the cabin and not be "squeezed." The lounge upstairs was spread out with plenty of couches and tables to work computers and photo processing. There was plenty of room for dinners either outside on the deck or inside in the lounge.

The Diving: Within the 16,500 islands of Indonesia there are over 600 types of coral and 3,000 species of fish. This phenomenal variety of creatures ensures that each dive is unique and exciting. Essentially, the Paradise Dancer picked us up at the north end of Sulawesi, sailed north for four days, and then sailed south for four days with the remaining days at the national park outside of Manado. Each location provided an opportunity to delve into the depths and photograph, or just enjoy, the changing scenery. As one who loves the interface between clown fish and sea anomies, the challenge to photograph the various combinations ensured fun on every dive.

A real challenge when faced with the clown fish was to have those little ones pose for your camera. The color variations of both the anomies and the fish assured challenges in focusing and color matching. A few "snaps" were taken to compare the black/yellow, grey/black, and orange/blue clown fish and the associated sea anomies. We especially liked the blue anomies and the brown/black clown fish. With two dives in the morning and two in the afternoon, everyone had multiple opportunities to "get wet" and challenge the camera environment. Within the ten days, there were eight night dives to satisfy the curiosity of the divers as to the nightlife of the coral reefs of Indonesia. Each dive was unique and each time we surfaced we exclaimed, "that was the best one yet!" The Dive Masters were expert in the dive sites and added significantly to our anticipation with their pre-dive briefings. The dive arrangements were excellent with individual baskets laid out under the benches on deck with plenty of room to hang our suits and skins. Each of the two dive tenders is structured to move you quickly from the ship to the dive location with quiet 200 horsepower 4-stoke engines. Entry into the water is easy with everyone rolling off simultaneously

A unique aspect of diving in Indonesia is the fact that it is in the "ring of fire" with volcanoes erupting and land movements occurring continuously in the region. We dove next to many active volcanic islands and experienced the fun of looking up at the mountaintop, realizing that is was an active volcano, and predicting when the next explosion was to occur (probably within the next 2,000 years – hopefully not in the next ten minutes). One special trip was on the third morning when the early wake-up call had us snorkeling in volcano-heated water. The steam coming off of the water at 0630 in the morning was a special sight as we approached the "hot tub" of the ocean. We all jumped into the normally warm water (84 degrees) and swam toward the steam. As we approached the warmer water we wandered between warm and hot spots. Once, we found a rock to stand on with a steady flow of hot water, we just stood there enjoying the lower back massage of swirling water that must have been between 100 and 102 degrees. If you could handle hotter water, you just went further toward the steaming water and stopped when it was "right for you." As we floated in the water we looked up at the top of the volcano and saw a long plume of smoke that was being highlighted by the rising sun on the far side of the island.

Each dive was special with four offered each day. The last ones were usually a dusk dive or a night dive depending on the positioning of the ship during the 10-day trip. The beauty of the coral triangle was evident on each dive and the colors were remarkable. All of the camera specialists were concentrating on the beauty of the colors and corals. The fish were small and the creatures varied. The nudibranchs and other animals ensured that photographers were happy with every dive. Periodically, there were wall dives with some current so that we could drift past the coral and just enjoy the scenery as we floated by. Small, beautiful, and colorful were the words that described the phenomenal reefs and animals as well as fish. As I was taking about 100 pictures each dive, the variety was amazing. Of course, the 100 pictures were usually culled down to 50 or so when out of focus, moving fish or just plain bad lighting interfered with the picture. Every photographer was remarking on their best pictures of a turtle, nudibranch, sea snake or sea anomie. Each was proud of the selection they ended up with at the end of the week.

The Crew: Once again the crew excelled at taking care of us. As we traveled around the boat, the crew ensured we were either being fed or getting ready for a dive. The dive bell keeps going off and you have to figure out if you are wet… you went to eat… if you were dry… you went to dive and get wet. The hot breakfasts were usually served after the first dive on the dive deck while the lunch was buffet and the dinner was multi course with soup. The spices were light and there were many choices. One night the miszo soup and tempura vegetables and shrimp even provided a Japanese taste and flair.

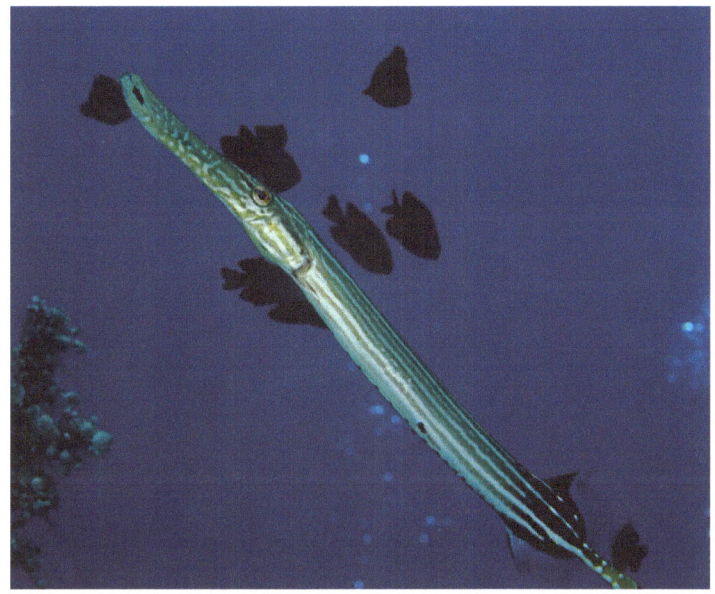

The cabins were cleaned by the time you returned from your first dive while the boat crews were ensuring that you had a great dive. The valet diving aspects were especially great with the lifting from the water of weights and BC prior to entering the boat. Essentially, all you had to worry about was your mask and camera, as the rest was loaded, filled and moved according to who was diving on what boat for which dive. In addition, the attitude of the crew ensured a pleasant experience with lots of smiles, and friendly banter.

TOP DIVE SPOTS[3]

The Paradise Dancer is a luxury live aboard three masted schooner which leaves North Sulawesi Island at the Lembeth Strait and explores Bangka Island, the Sangihe Island chain and the Bunaken National Marine Park. The general area allows for tremendous opportunities to swim among the colorful corals and boulders that shelter fish. These include snapper, surgeon fish and the ever present clownfish. The Sangihe Archipelago provides over a hundred miles of secluded, lush, volcanic islands. The deep ocean trench ensures the waters teems with multiple types of fish and natural environments that stimulate the mind and camera finger. There are rainforest on most of the islands with many active volcanoes such as Siau at 4,600 feet high. The morning opportunity to go snorkeling at Mahangetang, an active underwater volcano near Siau, is spectacular. Huge boulders are spread near the shore with multiple areas where tiny bubbles surface as gasses are released from underground seeps. One amazing realization is that this volcanic flow is creating another new island with all the benefits of new dive locations and sea life. The upwelling of deep water currents ensure plenty of food for the full range of fish and other underwater creatures. This

---

[3] Peter Hughes website on 18 Jan 09 is the source for the Top Dive Spots with the Paradise Dancer.

abundance of life ensures that each dive is worth exploring and keeping watch for new surprises such as dolphins and turtles.

The Bunaken National Marine Park was created in 1991 and spreads out on the west side of Sulawesi's north end. The 343 square mile habitat for tropical water creatures provides remarkable opportunities to explore while looking for black tip reef sharks, napoleon fish, and dugongs. Within the park, there are 22 official dive locations with protection of the environment as the principle objective while still enabling tourist diving. The beautiful coral and amazing fish life are superb for both wide angle and macro photography. There are the "shy critters" such as pygmy seahorses, mimic octopus, flamboyant cuttlefish, harlequin shrimp, skeleton shrimps, candy crabs, pegasus sea moths, and bobbit worms. Along with the usual reef fish there are also more unusual ones such as hairy frogfish, snake eels, stonefish, devilfish, sea robins, stargazers, devil fish and even the weedy scorpionfish. There are also beautiful seahorses including pygmies, pegasus, mandarinfish, ghost pipefish and the endemic banggai cardinalfish. The incredible array of nudibranchs come in all shapes and colors. This is the one location where you will likely encounter a species you have never seen before on every dive!

The chart on the next pages shows the area where the ship cruised. The adventure continued for all ten days and showed the passengers areas that they had only dreamed of. Can you imagine? Yes, we now can!

A Live-Aboard Example • 45

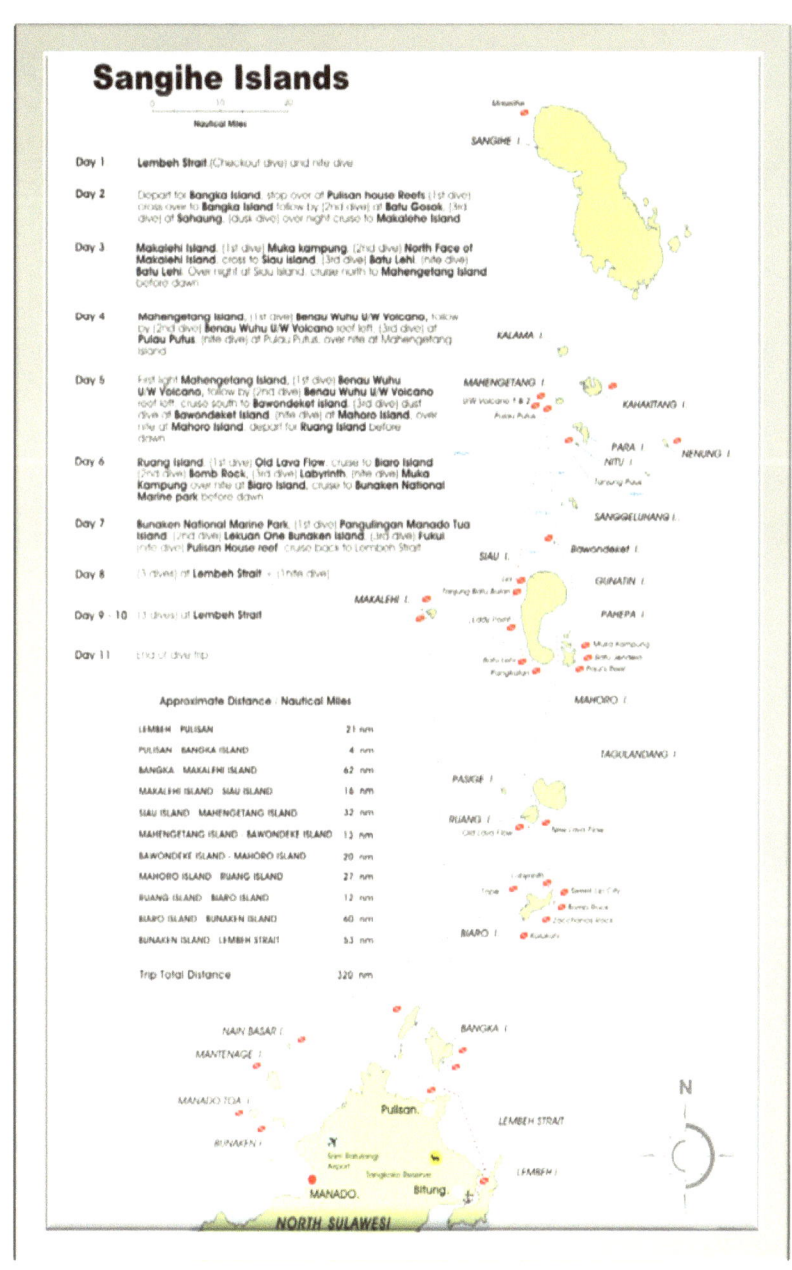

CHAPTER 6: PREPARATION FOR UNDERWATER PHOTOGRAPHY

INTRODUCTION

As you float beneath the surface of the water, slowly sipping the air from your tank, you see wonders inducing spectacular reactions. Small fish, swirling schools of fish, coral with all the colors of the rainbow, water -- blue with sunbeams streaking through fading away into the deep – all saturate you with emotions. All the images are captured in your mind. Then you surface and return to the reality of a world where birds, trees, flowers, sky, and clouds, again fill your mind. At this point you return to your job, the hustle and bustle of your neighborhood and friends and the press of your daily life. They all tend to suppress the wonders you have experienced on your SCUBA trip. Again, as you return to normalcy, you think, if I could only relive those moments and share with others. Well, you can. The world of photography provides us with the tools to retrieve those memories and share the wonders we have seen. One of the principal reasons we have gone on the underwater photo safari is to share these wonderful memories. Jacques Cousteau showed the world of wonders he was experiencing with the release of his first underwater (and French award winning) film, *18 Meters Deep*, in 1943, and with his first Academy Award winning film, *The Silent World*, in 1956. In both films he

shared the world's wonders he was seeing below the surface of the oceans. And, as they say, the rest his history. His still and motion photography was the catalyst that stimulated the SCUBA diving industry. And now, we all want to do what he did and capture what we see in photography so we can share the wonder with others.

Proficient SCUBA Photographic Steps: Advancements in technology now enable us all to become underwater photographers. If you follow our recommendations and checklist, you can prepare yourself to become the world's next Academy Award winning underwater photographer. The steps to becoming a proficient underwater photographer are simple and are shown in the next few pages.

>**Step 1: Learn to SCUBA dive, very-very well.**
>**Step 2: Master your camera on land.**
>**Step 3: Learn and become proficient at underwater photography**

Step 1: Learn to SCUBA dive, very-very well. To survive you must master all SCUBA skills. You must be comfortable being underwater and around fish, and things that crawl on the bottom of the ocean. To accomplish this you must learn and practice your SCUBA skills. You must be able to float motionlessly at any depth. If you are beating the water to death with your arms and legs flailing, you are not going to facilitate good pictures. Fish hate big things with lots of motion and will stay far away or go hide in the rocks. If you are constantly clearing your mask or adjusting your buoyancy you will miss the best photo opportunities of your life. In addition, if you do all the above SCUBA beginner behaviors, you will quickly run out of air. To become an excellent underwater photographer, SCUBA diving must be second nature to you. You must control yourself in an alien environment without thinking. And, don't forget, you are the lifeline for your dive buddy. Yes, in addition to thinking about your own well being, you must watch out for and, if necessary, take care of your buddy.

Some people spend their whole life learning how to become a good SCUBA diver and be comfortable in the water. Some will never be totally comfortable. But, when you find an experienced underwater photographer, you will have found a good SCUBA diver. Take the time to watch the photographer get their SCUBA gear ready. Look at all the equipment checks they are making. It only takes a moment; but, a good photographer checks the function and status of all equipment, twice. A malfunction or failed piece of SCUBA equipment makes for many missed photographs and a situation that may put them in danger – and maybe their dive buddy as well. A basic rule is – "If you are not comfortable SCUBA diving, do NOT take a camera into the water." Instead, practice your underwater skills. Poor SCUBA diving techniques do not improve if you are struggling with a camera. First master your SCUBA diving skills.

Step 2: Master your camera on land. Poor land photography skills do not translate to good underwater photography. However, a good land photographer can become a good underwater photographer. Another basic rule – "take time to learn and master all the buttons and settings on the display window." Study flash photography and learn how to use it and when it is not needed. Both situations will occur underwater. The best way to start learning how to handle your camera is to sit down and read the manual. Most people never do this and then get angry when things don't work the way they want. If you watch a master photographer, they will change camera settings almost by feel. They have read the manual and practiced changing settings with this particular camera. Some have put white tape on the outside of the housing and made notes and, in water proof ink, reminders – a brief underwater list that stays with the camera and is easy to find, read and use. Then, they will set the camera to be ready to take the next most likely shot, - macro, mid-range or wide angle. They will not be looking at the scene they want to photograph only to look away to the camera for the next few minutes to figure out how to get the camera set properly. They know exactly what settings they need and quickly make the changes, if any, to capture the photo. This skill of rapidly setting the camera is exactly what a SCUBA diver must be able to do underwater. And, this is in addition to keeping yourself and your buddy safe. Remember, safety first.

In addition to reading and understanding the camera manual, we suggest that you take a land photo class, maybe with your SCUBA camera out of the housing. Land photography skill classes are an excellent, and necessary, foundation for underwater photography. There are many good and inexpensive classes. Our favorites are the evening and weekend classes at the local schools. They are inexpensive and teach basic through advanced photography techniques. Go take them. Start at the entry level where in the first class they show you the camera front and the back and the top and the bottom. They show you were the batteries go and where memory cards go. They teach how to take photos and then how to get them out of your camera. The hardest part is that your best photos are critiqued in front of the class. A little daunting at first; but, this is how you learn to take better photos. Self critiques and critiques by others are part of becoming a good photographer. When you have taken all the classes you think you need and your photography skills are at a point where you think you are proficient, take more advanced classes and take more photos. Each time, striving to improve your skills. Remember, you are only competing against yourself. The photos you will be taking are for your personal enjoyment and for sharing with those you love. You do not need to become a world master land photographer; but, you must be the master of your camera. You must learn to operate it like you're touch typing on a typewriter (oops, computer keyboard).

Step 3: Learn and become proficient at underwater photography. This is the hard part. You are already a good SCUBA diver and no longer have to concentrate on SCUBA fundamentals. You are the master of your camera on land. Now you must combine these two skills into a new skill, underwater photography.

An underwater camera is similar to, but different than, a land camera. There is a strong protective case that keeps the water away from the camera and has little plungers and flippers that let you operate the buttons and dials on the camera. Similar to what you have become used to – but different. These underwater controls are bigger and closer together than you are used to; and, they don't look the same underwater as they do on land. In the dim underwater light the small function indicators fade below readability. There will be rubber cables with waterproof connectors that will pass electronic signals from your camera to your underwater strobe telling them when and how long to fire. On newer underwater cameras, the copper and rubber cables are replaced with fiber optics, a whole new dimension in technology. So what must you do??

Don't despair; you can master this new skill. You have mastered all things leading to this challenge, so keeping going. Don't give up. The **first** activity is to **read all the books** on underwater photography you can find. Use your local library. They will have an excellent selection of infrequently used books. Start with the books on composition and "how-tos." The books on camera and flash hardware will be interesting but out of date by several years. However, you can learn what problems you may encounter with underwater equipment and how to alleviate them. My favorite books are those by Cathy and Jim Church. They are still on my bookshelf and we regularly thumb through them. The underwater photography basics they teach are still valid. Learn them and you will be more than half way to becoming an excellent underwater photographer. Their first book, *Beginning Underwater Photography* was first published in 1972 and revised and republished several times. It is still a classic. They wrote and published several more, each time using the more advanced film cameras on the market but with the same classic underwater photography techniques. Go find good underwater photography books and read them. They have all the basic techniques you will need to know.

A **second** activity, but not my favorite, is to **take a class** on underwater photography. We find them expensive and not as instructional as you think – unless you take a very expensive class with personal attention. An alternative approach is the practice – practice – practice concept with self critique and feedback from friends. You can do as well by reading, doing, reviewing your photos, critiquing your photos, reading and then doing again. Only after you have done all your homework should you take your camera into a swimming pool. Do not take your camera underwater for the very first time in the open ocean. You will be asking for an unpleasant experience and, perhaps, an expensive lesson.

Consistent quality photographs mean you have reached a stable skill level and are ready to apply your artistic touch. Only then should you expand and look around you and see what others are doing and how well they are doing it. What techniques do they have for managing the camera that you may want to emulate? Maybe now would be a good time to take an underwater photography class to refine your skills and reach for the next level. The best land and underwater photographers in the world follow a classic method:

a. Prior to taking a photo, look at 100 good photos by others
b. Take your photo
c. Review your photo, then look at another 100 good photos by others

The above classic method will give you ideas and reference data to self critique your photos. You will find your photographs improving with each dive trip and each dive. If you follow this book, you will soon be the underwater photographer others are seeking to emulate. And in no time, you will be taking a good image of what you intended. Remember; watch your air, your depth, your dive time, and your buddy. No photo is worth risking your safety.

Equipment Preparation

The following two questions are vastly different and take you in unanticipated directions. In addition, the next few pages talk about lessons learned about underwater photo safaris.

Question 1 – what kind of camera should I get?
Question 2 – what is the best underwater camera on the market, for me?

Starter Set: Let's start with the real issue, money! A surprising point about underwater photography is everything costs a LOT of money. Most underwater cameras are a factor of 2 or more times as expensive as land photography equipment. If a simple point and shoot land camera cost $100 USD, the underwater housing may cost $200 - $300 USD. This does not count the external strobes you will probably want to go along with our camera. In addition, don't forget the fancy carrying case needed to protect your photographic gear. We are not talking about the simple soft sided back packs that may protect your equipment from slight scuffs but the military class hard sided cases that can withstand the gorilla in the airplane luggage compartments (my co-authors and I have never seen them but we hear them on every flight). When you get past the economical point and choose cameras of the fancy digital single lens reflex (DSLR) type, the cost really begin to skyrocket. A simple 10.5 mm wide angle Nikon lens used for taking panorama photos will cost about $550 USD. The wide angle port that enables you to use that lens on an underwater housing will cost $1,500-$3,000 depending upon the manufacture and other important bragging rights. How do you get around this dilemma when deciding if you want to be an underwater photographer? Simple – go cheap early and learn how to use the equipment. You can learn all the basic underwater photographic techniques with minimal equipment. You can upgrade to expensive and more capable equipment after you have decided you want to become an accomplished underwater photographer.

Our first book, in 2008, *Step Zero; Getting Started on a SCUBA Photo Trip*, has several pages and photos of equipment and a discussion of the decisions you will need to make prior to purchasing underwater photography equipment [http://www.lulu.com/content/2311454]. On page 49, you will see a photo of both a point and shoot and a DSLR that we took with us on the Grenada trip. What simply amazes people is that all the photos but two in the book were taken with the little point and shoot (on that trip, it was simply too rough to get a big DLSR into and out of the dive tender without risking damage). The camera used to take the photos, Pentax Optio 5Si, will actually fit into an Altoids mint can when it is out of the underwater housing. The Book #1 photos were taken with the camera's internal flash or natural light. No external strobes were used. Many of the images in this book were taken with point and shoot cameras. Take a look at the pictures. Not bad for such a little camera. In addition, think about the camera carrying case and support infrastructure for the larger cameras. Both camera types work, but the attributes and demands are different.

A very good and inexpensive underwater camera outfit may be purchased for about $1,000. We suggest a start with a simple camera with the manufacturer's underwater housing and one external manufacturer's strobe. Sea and Sea, SeaLife, Canon, Sony, Olympus and others all have cameras that will serve you well. For a little more money and a wider range of available cameras, one option is an Ikelite (Ikelite.com) housing and a single external strobe. The Ikelite housings will cost a little more; but, they are more durable and will provide you several more options. Two strobes provide better lighting options than one but are bulky. We recommend mastering a single strobe first. You will be able to buy a second strobe later.

An early determination you need to make about yourself is: do you really want to be an underwater photographer? Our recommendation is don't spend a lot of money experimenting with this new hobby. Many of us have closets full of unused sports equipment that we purchased prior to thinking and learning. You don't want to add an expensive underwater camera to the pile. We recommend a basic camera, simple housing, an external flash and a macro lens.

Megapixels: Don't get caught up in the race. There are few cameras on the market now with less than five megapixels. Anything with five or more megapixels will serve you well. The camera we used in our first book had five megapixels. You can make excellent 8 x 10 inch prints with five megapixels. There is an argument that says if you have a lot of megapixels you can crop more out of the photo and still have high resolution images left. Our preferred option is to get closer to your subject. All professional photographers will advise you to do all your cropping in the camera. And we agree with them. Fill the frame as you would like to see your final photo. The majority of new cameras are in the range of 8 to 10 megapixels.

Used equipment: This can be a good choice for beginners. If you know an underwater photographer who is upgrading their equipment, you may be able to buy their old equipment at an excellent price. Used equipment from someone you know is better than buying used equipment on eBay. We have purchased several items on eBay and have had very few problems; however, the equipment from friends comes with the history and someone who will help you learn how to use it and properly care for it. They will be able to pass along any attributes and limitations. If they are upgrading their equipment, they will be able to tell you why they think an upgrade for them is necessary. It is usually because they have grown their underwater photography skills to a point where they need more capable equipment. Or, they may just want newer equipment so they will have bragging rights. Many people want the newest and most expensive equipment just so they can brag. Few  photographers are capable of taking advantage of all the capabilities of the most expensive equipment. Really good photographers can use "average" equipment and depend upon their photographic skills to win the photo contest. Do not discard the idea of buying used equipment for your first underwater camera. It can be an excellent starter system to let you determine if you really want to be an underwater photographer without spending a lot of money.

Dreaming is good: We love to read all the photography magazines and find all the internet sites that recommend camera equipment. However, this is an expensive hobby – or worse yet – a VERY expensive hobby. Envision yourself underwater taking photos. Visualize the once in a lifetime moment with you capturing it in a world-class image. This is fun. But you also have to visualize how you are going to carry all this equipment and how you are going to pay for it. When you are making your camera wish list, don't forget to have a column for size and weight. After you have completed your list, you will soon need a LARGE and HEAVY travel case. Don't forget to visualize how you are going to pack and carry or check (shudder) this equipment on the airplane. You need to include all of the support items in this visualization. The cables, batteries, lubricants, and spare parts must all be included. You are going to need all of these things so don't skimp on your list. You need to be realistic with your expectations. Others manage to do it; so can you. Go buy your underwater camera.

Test Procedure (TP)

The next series of paragraphs will discuss test procedures (TP's) that have been proven to transition an embryonic photographer into a confident underwater photographer. These are:

>   TP 1 – **Take pictures at home with all parts assembled**
>   TP 2 – **Test housing in water without camera**
>   TP 3 – **Put camera in housing into water (pail or tub)**
>   TP 4 – **Take pictures in a bucket**
>   TP 5 – **In a pool, SCUBA and photography practices.**

TP 1 – Take pictures at home with all parts assembled. Start learning about your camera by putting all the parts together and take photos around the house and yard with your new camera in its underwater housing. You don't need water at this stage to learn how the camera works. The last thing you want to happen on a dive boat in a remote location is to take the camera and strobe out of the factory box for the first time. If you do this, you are doomed for disappointment and/or failure. Not only will you be unskilled with the equipment, we suspect you will be short a key part. We have seen this happen many times. Practice what you have learned in your readings. SCUBA diving magazines have frequent articles on how to take care of your underwater camera and how to take photos. READ them and practice what they are saying. They are teaching you the basics and you will need them.

> ### Memorable Events – Old Equipment Produces Great Photos
>
> In 2003, most SCUBA divers were changing or had changed to digital. Not me, I was still using my 1978 Nikonos-III with a 15mm lens, a 25 year old camera – older than some people on the boat. My slide film was processed on the boat and by mid-week, I was fielding questions like, "What kind of camera is that and how does your camera takes great photos?" My old photo equipment was outperforming the very expensive cameras in very expensive housings. The moral of the story is to learn to use what you have and learn to use it well!

TP 2 – Test housing in water without camera. Once you have taken images of the cat and flowers and your foot (don't laugh, we all have these) take your underwater camera housing, WITHOUT the camera in the housing, into the **water**. Make certain the housing is properly sealed and sink it underwater for a time. Watch for leaks. Watch for bubbles. Watch for things that don't look right. If you don't have access to a pool, a bucket of water or a bathtub will work just fine. If you don't see leaks or flooding, move on to the next step. Put your camera into the housing.

TP 3 – Put camera in housing into water (pail or tub). You just don't want your first flood to be on your first dive with your new camera. Its better to see a housing leak in a bucket where you can quickly remove it and determine what is causing the leak. Now put your camera into your underwater housing. Follow the manufacturer's directions. Make certain you have cleaned and properly lubricated the O-rings and put them in per direction. Close the housing. Close the latch. Make certain it locks into place. Look at the O-rings for kinks. Take several photos of things above water to prove all is working well. And, now, get ready for the BIG test. Yes, you will be as anxious as a kitten without a litter box; but, you must do it – put your new, expensive underwater camera into the water. Don't worry, if you followed the manufacture's direction, you will be fine. But, be cautious. Again, look for leaks, flooding or bubbles. If all is well, you can put your heart back in its proper place. Remember, there are two kinds of underwater photographers:

1. Those who have flooded a camera, and,
2. Those who are going to flood a camera.

TP 4 – Take pictures in a bucket. Once you have accomplished the "**dunk test,**" you are ready to go to the next step. Turn the camera on and take a photo of the bottom of the bucket or tub. The photo will not be memorable, but you will determine if the functions are working properly. Put a coin in the bottom of the bucket and take a picture of it. See if the camera's auto focus works. See if you can actually properly frame the coin in the viewfinder display on the back of the camera. See if the exposure is anywhere close to what you expected. All these are the skills you can practice without spending thousands of dollars on a SCUBA trip. If you can take good images of a coin in the bottom of a bucket, you are well on your way to becoming an underwater photography pro.

Remember what you have just done. You need to do this "rinse tank" or bucket test **every time** before taking your camera into the ocean. It is not a perfect test; but, it will find the "simple and stupid" errors that cause flooding. It is less dangerous to your camera to become damp with freshwater than to be completely flooded with salt water for many minutes under pressure. Once salt water penetrates into your camera's batteries and electronics with the power on, the electronics turn to junk. You can just put your camera into the trash. The underwater housing may be saved, once you determine the cause of the flooding, but your camera is lost. The freshwater dunks are a practice you should standardize! When on the live aboard, the camera rinse tub is the perfect place to do this before each salt-water dive. [note: a freshwater flooding is recoverable whereas a salt-water flooding is almost always catastrophic.]

TP 5 – In a pool, SCUBA and photography practices. The final step in preparation is to put on your SCUBA gear and test the camera in a pool. Many try to skip this step even at the risk of losing their cameras. The first time you are underwater, with a camera, you will find out you have a LOT of things going on. Yep, you must adjust your buoyancy while holding your camera. Yep, you must adjust your BC while holding your camera. Yep, you must . . . . The list goes on. However, it is better to learn how to SCUBA and manage your camera in a safe place, then in the middle of the ocean. You don't want to be 5,000 miles from home in the middle of tropical islands struggling with your camera when you should be taking images of things dreams are made of.

The culmination of these test procedures leads to a SCUBA vacation with your small camera which will be a pleasure. You will not only be able to capture the moment in photos but you will have something you can easily carry with you onto the airplane. If and when you check your camera, you begin to imagine luggage gorillas jumping on it just as you sit back into your seat. If we can, we always pack our cameras into small, well padded, bags and carry it on. Include the strobe too. Other things, such as your chargers and batteries in their individual plastic cases, can all go into the checked bags. If you lose them, you can probably replace them when you get to your location. Because, of course, you have followed the recommendations in this book and have extra days in your vacation area to go shopping and buy these more common items. Remember, when you get to your location, put your equipment all together and check its functionality. What works at home may not work at your vacation area. It's not clear what traveler's law Murphy was involved in, but we have experienced it all.

If you can afford it, take **two cameras**, one camera for underwater photography and one for surface photography. If they are the same kind of camera, you will have a full backup if one fails. If the cameras are different, I recommend an underwater housing for both. Yes, this is more expensive;

but, there is nothing as disappointing as having your only underwater camera fail the first day and doing without a toy to play with for the rest of the vacation. The other children will be having all the fun with their underwater cameras. If you purchased small point and shoot cameras, this will be a manageable logistics problem. Again, into a small backpack or carrying case and on to the plane they go. If you have multiple DSLRs with many large housings and strobes, you will need to submit your photo equipment as checked baggage. In addition, many times you will have to pay an overweight or extra bag charge. These can really add up if you take a lot of equipment. The pros know what they are doing and experience this all the time. To them, it is the cost of doing what they love. So, after you have selected a reasonably priced underwater point and shoot camera, what next?

Preparing for First Camera Dive:

Now that you are at your vacation location and on the ocean, leave your camera on the boat for your first dive. This will probably be the first dive you have done in awhile and you need to concentrate on refreshing your SCUBA skills and making certain your SCUBA equipment is ready to support you. As you marvel at the new surroundings, practice your underwater photography skills, such as buoyancy control and buddy safety. Again, it is amazing how many items fail in the closet or on the flight. Regulators are the worst. NEVER get your regulator serviced and then put it onto an airplane without trying the regulator on a few local dives. A regulator that works in the repair shop may not work under full SCUBA conditions. Most failed regulators have "just come out of the repair shop." Yep, we hear it almost every trip. Once you have a dive or two under your belt on this trip, and you are certain all your SCUBA gear functions properly, you are now ALMOST ready to take your camera into the big bad ocean. You are asking for trouble until you verify your SCUBA equipment works and you and your buddy are acclimated to this diving area.

> ### Memorable Event(s) – Second Camera Saves Disaster
>
> Five times in the past seven years I have loaned my spare underwater camera to a person on the boat who flooded theirs. Each time the flood occurred in the first 3 camera dives and was caused by rushing and not doing the pre-dive assembly and checks properly. I was teased because I had packed two underwater cameras but not after I loaned them out. I had saved their very expensive SCUBA vacation from turning into a disaster. I won't embarrass Diane, Jerry, Derek, Peter or Dennis by giving their full names; however, I still get thank you cards from them. The morals are 1) do your pre-dive checks religiously and 2) if you can afford it, take a second underwater camera, it can prevent a disastrous trip.

Your first open ocean dive with your new photo equipment should be housing only, WITHOUT camera. This will give you confidence and verify that your housing seals and functions properly. To do this, prepare your housing as you would for a dive if the camera was in the housing; and, verify it will withstand the pressure at dive depth. This is good to do on your second dive. The **first dive verifies** your SCUBA skills are tuned-up and your **equipment** works. The **second dive verifies** your **housing** is water-tight at depth. The following steps and check list are the same ones you should use with your camera in your housing. Use them on this second dive as a practice. However, before you take the big step, ask yourself the following questions to ensure you and your equipment are prepared.

	Question to Ensure Preparation is Complete
1	Is the camera properly seated in the housing?
2	Are all the ports, caps, plugs and clasps properly closed?
3	Are the O-rings sealed properly or pinched and sticking out?
4	Have you done your camera functional test? [dive deck photo?]
5	Have you tested your housing into the rinse tank and checked for leak?
6	Have you looked for leaks (bubbles)? None?

Memorable Events – Paradise Dancer camera room

One of the divers who had a very expensive DSLR camera rig (new Nikon D300, new Sea&Sea housing and 2 Sea&Sea Duo YS0120 strobes) set up his camera one night and was almost in tears the next morning. He had forgotten to pack the sync cord for his photo rig – he could not take photos with his strobe. This is very-very bad for taking macro photos and most wide angles.

Solution: Dennis loaned him a pair of sync cords. The only ones within many miles that would fit and work.

Moral: use the check list when packing (hook up all your gear to operational configuration and do an operational check to see that it all works as expected. Then pack it all) Michael did not do this and had it not been for the resourceful Dennis and Pete dive team, he would NOT HAVE had an enjoyable photo safari.

First Camera Dive

After you and your camera pass the above steps, you are ready to go into the water. When you get to your dive site and you are instructed to get into the water, you get into the water WITHOUT your camera. Leave it on the boat and let one of the experienced boat people pass your camera to you, gently. Don't worry, he won't let go of it until you have a firm grasp of it and signal to him that you have it (the reverse is true getting out of the water). He has done this many times. He is a professional – trust him. Now for a SCUBA industry wide question with no common answer.

-Question - Do you attach the camera to you with some kind of a strap or just keep it free in your trusty hands???
-Answer - Both methods work.

We normally use a small wrist strap with our point and shoot because the camera is so small that we could easily drop it. In addition, my camera hand has been stung by the coral as we are reaching under or around the coral to get a world-class photo. An unexpected sting or scrape will make you flinch and jerk your hand away. The wrist strap will ensure your camera comes back with your hand. We have recently incorporated a stainless steel, 18 inch, stick to use in the other hand as a tool to protect the reef. If you use the stick as a lever on rock (and watch out for those sneaky rock fish) you will not flutter around for the photo or scrape the coral with your fins or tank; nor will you stir up the sediment and mess up the image.

IMPORTANT RULE – Don't talk and assemble

If someone interrupts you while you are assembling your photo equipment, stop what you are doing and talk to the person. Then, when you are finished with the interruption, restart the assembly and functional check process from the beginning. Never assume you know where you left off and never assemble when you are talking. You are not as competent as you think you are. Similarly, never talk with an underwater photographer when they are putting their equipment together for a dive. They are trying to concentrate on the assembly and making all the necessary checks. If you interrupt them, they will be polite and respond to you, and maybe chat a little; but then, they have lost all sense of where they were in the camera assembly process.

With the DSLR, we don't use a strap. No cord or bungee connecting my BC to my housing or strobe arms. Some folks do but we find we are usually holding on to the camera with both hands most of the time and doing very well. This could be a mistake but this is what I find most comfortable. If we are in shallow water, and drop the camera, we will just pick it up. If we are in the great deep blue and drop it, we will get to buy new equipment. We argue this point all the time with no resolution. To close on this topic, as you are using our recommended P&S, attach it to you with a wrist strap when you are starting your dive and remove it when you are exiting the dive. You don't need a long strap; the eight inch strap that comes with the housing will work fine.

Once you are in the water with your camera on your first camera dive, floating on the surface, ready to descend, it is time to **locate your dive buddy**. Yep, all your mental energy is focused on your expensive camera and you have lost sight of your dive buddy. Do not descend until you find your buddy. UW photographers are the worst in the world for getting separated from their buddy and diving alone. This is very dangerous for both you and for your dive buddy. When you are at diving depth, enjoying the new toy you have to capture the beauty you are seeing; but, you must stay linked to your dive buddy. You will have a tendency to become too focused on your subject and totally ignore your buddy. If your buddy is a photographer, they also may become totally focused and lose track of you. If they are not a photographer, they may become bored with what you are doing and just decide to move on a little bit, then a little bit more, then they are out of sight and range to help you if needed. Stay together; you are each other's lifeline.

Before First Picture: The next six steps seem simple; but, they are perfect for your first photos. They will keep you and your buddy safe and let you get maximum enjoyment out of your first underwater photography experience. You should be able to take a few photos that you can be proud of and show to your friends. That is important. If you recall the first part of this chapter, one of the principle reasons to be an underwater photographer is to show your friends the wonders you see while SCUBA diving. Yes, you are now a fledging Jacque Cousteau. Be proud of yourself. You are doing somethiing very few will ever do.

REMEMBER: When you are on the bottom ready to take photos, do you know where your **dive buddy** is? Don't forget to keep track of your buddy.

The **First Step on the bottom** is to make certain you are safe and not going to damage anything (reef, yourself, life forms, etc). I recommend first timers find a spot on the sand next to a coral head with several sponges on it. Once on the sand, again look at your housing to see if it is still water tight. Do this at every opportunity. Cameras can flood anytime. A good bump on the reef may cause an O-ring to dislodge and start a flood. A slow leak can take quite a long time to fill the housing. There may be sufficient time for you to locate your buddy, and start a slow controlled assent to the surface with proper safety stops. Once back on the surface prepare to re-enter the boat. During this whole period, you should be keeping your camera oriented so the water stays in the bottom of the housing away from the camera. If the camera stays dry, you have a good chance of saving it. More on this topic later.

Macro, or close up photography, is highly recommended **for beginners**. Good results are more easily achieved – providing lots of personal rewards that you are mastering this new skill. Macro underwater photography is very rewarding and more likely to produce photos that are self gratifying and that you will be proud to show your friends. Taking photos of things that do not move, or do not move fast, enables you to concentrate on improving and perfecting your photographic skills (vice chasing fish all over the ocean). Remember, they are at home in the ocean and you are just a visitor. When you chase after a fish, all you will probably get is a picture of the tail. You will remember it as fun but this is not the photo you will want to show your friends. Don't worry, all of us have hundreds of photos of fish tails (perhaps our next book will include a collection of them).

The **Second Step** is to turn your camera on and configure it to take a photo. Take a test photo of anything. Your fin is usually near you and makes an excellent close range subject. If your fin photo turns out well, then look for a subject on the coral head. We usually recommend a nice, colorful, small size sponge with a nice, plain, blue water background. Why a sponge? They don't move and they make beautiful photos. In addition, because they don't move, you can change your camera settings and work on picture composition. I make light of this; but, you are in the process of learning how to run your new underwater camera and you need to concentrate on learning how to operate the camera in the ocean. So, find a nice subject on a coral head next to a patch of sand. Kneel on the sand and get ready to do your thing. And, **take the photo of your dreams!**

The **Third Step on the bottom** is to close in on your subject and compose it properly. This action should be consistent with the way you learned on land and read in the underwater photography books. Make certain you are the correct distance from your subject for your strobe configuration and the strobe is properly placed to minimize back scatter, and take your photo.

The **Fourth Step** is to back off from your subject and take a look at the photo displayed on the back of your camera and enjoy your achievement. You have probably done very well if you have prepared yourself for this experience. Do your own photo critique and take a second photo of your sponge making necessary adjustments to get a better photo. Was the subject properly lit? Can you see the colors? Is there backscatter? Did you get what you wanted in the photo? Is the background simple and not detracting from your subject? Is the water in the background blue, black, white or washed out? Kneeling on the sand is an excellent place to critique your work. You are in a safe location. You are not going to plunge to the depths nor rocket to the surface. Your buddy will know where you are and you can look around and find your buddy prior to taking your next photo. You are not going to trash the reef with your fins or get scratched or stung by the coral. Take your time reviewing your photos. Evaluate what improvements are needed. Make camera adjustments if needed.

The **Fifth Step on the bottom** is to take a photo of the sponge again. Is the photo better? Did your composition and equipment adjustment make the changes you expected? Take as many photos as necessary to get a good sponge photo. When you are satisfied, find a new subject on the coral head. Look for a nudibranch, an anemone or a shrimp and then start this five step process all over again.

The **Sixth Step and final step** is to locate your buddy and jointly agree to return to the surface when, or before, your air reaches the return point. Don't be surprised it you have used air at a higher rate than you normally do. You have been excited, doing things you have not done before, and your heart and respiratory rate have been elevated. Don't worry, as you gain experience, you will return to your normal air consumption rate. When you reach the surface, turn your camera off and check for leaks. Many cameras have been known to flood as the water pressure has lessened and the O-rings have relaxed. Keep the camera ready to take photos on your way to the surface. It is quite common for a rare fish to swim by and want its photo taken. Another common item is to take photos of your dive buddy while you are doing your safety stop. All buddies love photos of themselves and will ask to see them as soon as you are on the boat; and then, they ask for a copy. When you reach the surface, pass your camera to the person in the boat and climb in. You have now completed your first underwater photo experience. Wasn't it GREAT! But you are far from done. Here is the set of steps that ensured safe and proficient photography underwater.

First Step – make certain you are safe and not going to damage anything
Second Step – turn your camera on and configure it to take a photo.
Third Step -- close in on your subject and compose it properly.
Forth Step – back off from your subject and take a look at the photo on your camera
Fifth Step – take a photo of the sponge again.
Sixth Step – locate your buddy and jointly agree to return to the surface

AFTER THE DIVE

As soon as you can, put your underwater camera into a freshwater rinse tank. A good dive boat will have them easily available. You do not want the salt water to dry on your equipment as it will leave salt deposits that you will find almost impossible to remove. They will discolor your housing, cover your lens, and cause your buttons to stick. A reputable SCUBA operation will have a freshwater rinse tank ready for your immediate use. There is a social protocol for the rinse tank. Put your equipment in it as quickly as you can but take your turn. If you can, leave your camera in the tank to soak. Watch out for other cameras that may be in the tank soaking. Do not drop your camera on top of their cameras. Cameras have been known to flood as the equipment bangs against each other. This is in addition to possibly scratching the optical ports. Be considerate of others. Share the rinse tank and watch out for your equipment.

Camera table etiquette is paramount for an enjoyable SCUBA photo trip. As you took your camera out of the rinse take, you should have dried it with a towel. Do not take the air-hose you find at many SCUBA facilities and attempt to blow the water off. It is disturbingly noisy, it is not as effective as using a towel, and it will blow dirt and sand onto places where you will not be able to get it out. When you, your hair, and your camera are dry, it is time to open the underwater housing. Place your housing on a towel on a flat surface with the lid that opens facing the towel. When you unlatch and open the lid cover, you will find that water droplets will be under the lid with the O-ring and you do NOT want these droplets falling into the insides of your camera housing and getting onto your delicate camera equipment and electrical connections. In addition, make certain your face, hair and body are dry when working with your camera equipment. If you are wet, the water droplets will certainly fall into the inside of your housing, again causing damage. Remove your camera and put it into a plastic bag to protect it from other divers. Protect your camera. When you have serviced your housing by removing and cleaning and re-lubing your O-rings, close it, keeping the O-rings in place and unwanted items from entering the housings. If you have been using an underwater strobe, leave it alone until you reinstall the camera into the housing.

SAVING YOUR PHOTOS

Next, you must take your camera back to your room, remove the memory card, and transfer the photos from the card to your computer. When the images are in your computer, make a duplicate copy. Mark the transfer from the card MASTER and mark the copy you just made WORKING COPY. Put the master in a consistent and safe location. NEVER WORK, LOOK or ADJUST your master copies. Work only from a "working" copy. This way, you can always go back to your master copy, make another duplicate and work from that new duplicate. Yes, you will find yourself unintentionally trashing a photo because of the things you do to it. It is important you keep the master pristine. Now that you have TWO copies on your laptop, get your external thumb drive or portable hard drive and put a copy of your MASTER photos onto this drive. If you have your photos on only one hard drive you are at risk. Hard drives fail (and at the worst possible moment) and will take your most precious photos to never-never land. Writing your MASTER photos to a CD or data DVD is also acceptable but a slower process. Once you have two copies of your photos on different storage devices, you may now look at the WORKING COPY of your photos to your heart's content.

Look at your photos to see the wonders you have captured. Now is the time to share with others. Also perform a self-critique of your photos. Ask yourself, what were you trying to capture in your image, what did you achieve, and what will you do differently next time. When you have looked at all your photos, make a copy for show. Everyone on the boat will want to see what you did. All divers are like that; but, photographers are the worst of the bunch. They want to see what the competition can do. I have never been on a boat where someone is not looking over your shoulder at photos you have just taken. Or, asking you how you did and did you get any good ones. They expect an answer. So, pick your best few (2 or 4) photos from the 100 that you took and only show those. Do NOT show your junk. They are only for you. When people look at only your good photos, they will think you are really an expert. By the end of the week you will have a 100 or so excellent images for show. You can then take these photos and pick the best. Select no more than 10 to 15 images. This may seem overly harsh but it is what the pros do. Show only your best.

You will have other underwater photo opportunities; and, after a few trips, you will have an impressive collection. You have not lost any of your photos. You love them all and do not want to delete them – so don't. Keep them safe so you can look at them; but, keep them to yourself. It is hard to accept; but, your friends will tire after looking at ten or so pictures. Your poor photos lead to excellent self critique, but really serve no other purpose. Your friends and strangers will only want to see your best. After you have downloaded your photos to your computer, made a duplicate working copy, and put a copy of your master image file on a second storage device, you are now ready to return to servicing your camera.

Find your freshly and fully charged batteries for your camera and strobe and return to your camera working area. Put fresh batteries into your camera and your external strobe. Reassemble your underwater camera to its underwater operating condition. Examine it carefully. Look for things that don't fit correctly. If the latches closed differently, open them and look for something that is not fitting properly or pinched. Perform a fully functional check. Take a photo of something on the camera table. See if the photo is what you expect.

Getting Ready for your Next Photo Dive

When you are satisfied that you have done all that you can do with your equipment prior to taking it back into the ocean, it is now time to reformat the memory card while in the camera. You have fresh batteries – now you want to ensure you have sufficient room on your camera memory card for your next dive. It is frustrating to find that your memory card is full while underwater. You then have to spend precious time and air during your dive to delete your old photos. Installing a new, unused memory card for each dive is even better. Keeping all your images on your memory cards (in addition to your two hard drive copies) is the best of all worlds. Memory cards are cheap. So, buy a lot of small ones or several large ones. You cannot have too many backup copies of your photos. When in doubt, backup, backup, backup. The same is true of your SCUBA equipment. You cannot have too much backup and safety equipment.

Remember, if someone starts to talk to you, stop what you are doing, put your camera down and continue with your conversation. When completed, return to your camera and start the servicing and assembly from the very beginning. Do not assume you know were you were in the assembly process when you were interrupted. Chances are you will remember incorrectly. So, assemble your equipment from the beginning. You will then know you have it right.

When satisfied that your camera functions properly, it is time to take it to a rinse tank. Not to rinse but to do a leak test. No, the tank is not very deep but it is all you have to check underwater integrity. I have seen many camera floods that could have been detected in a rinse tank. It is a simple check, and does not take much time, but will save you a lot of pain and anguish if a leak is identified. When your camera is fully serviced and ready for a dive, it is now time for you to relax and chat with your fellow divers. Or, take a nap. Remember to rehydrate yourself. You have taken care of you camera equipment; now, you need to take care of yourself. Other divers will be resting and not servicing their equipment. When they get around to it, they will find themselves rushed and will make errors. If a person floods a camera on your trip, there is a high likelihood they rushed through the camera servicing process and made an error. Don't rush; practice what you have properly taught yourself. It will pay many dividends.

Flooded Camera – What to Do?

A short note is needed on what to do if you find water seeping into your camera housing while on a dive. First, return to the surface **with your buddy** as safely and quickly as you can. Keep your housing so the water stays away from your camera. Do your **safety stop**. Do not skip this step. A camera can be replaced. You cannot. When you reach the boat, tell the boat person your problem prior to passing your camera to them. Tell them how you want it held prior to passing the camera to them. Get yourself and your dive buddy into the boat. At this time, open the housing a crack and let the water drain out. If the sea water has not reached and entered the camera or battery, you have an excellent chance of saving your camera. If your housing is half flooded and there is black sludge sloshing around, you are toast and have lost your camera.

If your camera is only damp, take it to a very, very dry and warm place, towel it off, remove the memory card and remove the battery. Open all the little battery, memory card and electrical card doors and put it someplace to dry. Do NOT take the air hose and blow into the camera. All you will do is blow water deeper into the inner workings causing damage. If you brought desiccant on the trip with you, put the camera into a plastic bag with the desiccant and again put the bag in a warm dry place. The compressor and engine rooms on a boat are excellent places. If you are at a land resort, the top of the TV is an excellent place. We have returned many cameras thought to be lost with the preceding procedure. We carry extra desiccant and plastic bags just for this process. We have made many friends for life by resurrecting their cameras. After you have serviced the camera, return to the housing and determine what caused the leak. Don't use the housing again until you know the cause. If necessary, repair the housing and take on a dive WITHOUT the camera. If it works properly, you may trust it with your camera. If it leaks again, you did not find the problem and you need to examine it again and find the cause. Continue to dive with the housing only, no camera, until it works properly. If it does not flood, you can try diving with the camera in the housing.

DIVING IS DONE

Now that you have had a fantastic SCUBA trip, it is time to put your camera way. Sad as it is to pack your equipment, NOW is the time to get it ready for your next trip. You generally must spend 24 hours on the surface prior to flying. This is more than sufficient time to clean both your SCUBA equipment and your underwater photography equipment. Give everything a good soak and rinse in freshwater. If it moves, you may want to lube it with a wide variety of silicones that are available for that purpose. Then give it a good drying. While your SCUBA equipment is drying, work on your camera equipment. Take the housing apart as much as you can. Remove the O-rings from everything. Do NOT store your O-rings in the housing's operational grooves. If you do, they will be compressed until your next dive and may not provide the elasticity they need to perform their sealing functions; and, your housing may flood. Inspect them for cuts, tears or pinches. Make certain they are clean. Give them a light coating of the manufactures recommended lubricant and place them into a small plastic bag. The bag will keep them clean. Then take a small slip of paper and write the date of this dive trip and put it into the bag with the O-rings. This way you can keep track of how many dive trips you have on this set of O-rings. Do not trust yourself to remember. You need lots of data reminders and check lists. There are too many details to trust to your memory. If the O-rings are in good condition and you think you can use them on the next trip, put this plastic bag of O-rings into the housing and close the housing. This keeps them from getting lost and protects them from getting pinched. If your slip of paper has several dive trips on this set of O-rings or they are getting several years old, you should replace them. O-rings are consumable items. They do NOT last forever and, compared to a new camera, they are cheap. So, don't skimp on the O-rings.

> **Memorable Events – CAMERA FLOODING**
>
> On the 1st dive of the day, a diver started his dive and was about ten feet below the surface when he noticed water was entering his Ikelite housing. He rose to the surface, boarded the dive tender and returned to the Paradise Dancer. Investigation of the cause revealed that one of the internal control arms was in the wrong position and stopped the back from properly seating the O-ring. This condition could have been prevented. He was usually very cautious and assembled his camera and tested for water tightness in the camera rinse tank the night prior to the dive. On this day, he failed to do that. He assembled his camera the morning of the dive and did not allow sufficient time for visually inspecting the watertight O-ring seals and testing seal integrity in the rinse tank. This unseated O-ring would have been caught by a quick dunk in the rinse tank or by visually checking the O-ring seating. His rush nearly cost him an expensive camera.
>
> Moral: Take your time assembling your underwater photo equipment and perform any test you can including a camera rinse tank leak test prior to taking your camera on a dive.

Now place your camera, your housing, your strobe(s), your spare parts, your batteries, your chargers . . . . . EVERYTING into its travel case or luggage. Look around your dive area, your room, the camera room, and the places on deck where you were. Leave nothing. Then go find the folks you loaned things to. Get them back and pack them. After you have packed all of your SCUBA and photo equipment, it is nice to kick back and enjoy the remaining hours of your trip.

End of trip Check list

During the last hours of your trip is the best time to work on your end of trip check list. Things that happened are fresh in your mind so write them down.

-What worked well?
-What didn't work well?
-What lessons did you learn?
-What do you want to accomplish next time?
-What equipment do you want to have next trip? Same? Different?

These are the things that go through your mind but you need to write them down. During the discussions at your last dinner you will think of many things, your friends will think of many things, and, there will be NO time in the morning. The last morning is too busy with final packing and saying goodbyes. When you have your computer out and are swapping photos with new friends, make certain you get their addresses and make a list of the things you promised them and that they promised you. While on your computer, work on our checklist. If you don't do this list now, you will miss many items you really want to accomplish. The action and equipment list at the end of this book will give you an excellent starting place for what to put on this "end of trip" check list. It is easy to scan as you are watching the final sunset with your buddies. It is also a good starter for conversation. What are their thoughts? What are they going to do? What do they wish they had done differently; and, what would they do the same?

Reminders for the Photo Pro

Most thoughts in this book are directed at amateur photographers and adventurers. However, there are two check list items for the professional that should be pointed out to the amateur. The first is a model release and the second is the CBP Form 4457, Certificate of Registration for Personal Effects Taken Abroad. The amateur can normally defer both items; but, as you progress to the pro level, they will become very important to you.

Model Release: As you photograph fish and coral underwater, the subject really don't care if you use their photos in a commercial manner. Unidentifiable SCUBA divers in the distance also fall into the same category as fish. But, when you take photos of people close enough to be identified, you should consider having them sign a model waver prior to using their photo in a commercial publication. This practice is common in the photography world and protects both the photographer and model. As money becomes involved, the release (and perhaps a contract for pay) becomes very important. Excellent examples and discussions may be found on the internet by doing a search for "model waver."

CBP Form 4457: When you are a tourist, traveling to remote locations, it is almost expected that you will have a camera hung around your neck. As your desire to take more and more photo and computer equipment in and out of a wide variety of countries and cultures, customs officers will determine if the equipment is an import/export item for resale. There is no stated equipment limit that may fall into this category; but, we have heard that some photographers experienced complications at border check points. If your equipment now requires several large professional shipping cases (and/or you must pay extra shipping charges) you can expect to be interviewed relative to commercial endeavors. To document that the equipment belongs to you and intended for your use and will not be sold, the Customs and Border Protection Service has produced a very simple form to document ownership and your intention to return with it. It also shows the Customs that you did not buy it overseas but brought it from home. You will avoid paying import duty charges on equipment that you already own. The form is very simple (only requiring a simple description), but must be registered at the Customs office at the airport PRIOR to you departure. It only takes a moment and can be done ahead of time.

Conclusion

The end of an underwater photography experience rewards you with two key items.

- **First** is **enjoyment** of all the small wonders you have captured in pictures.
- **Second** is **sharing** the photos of these wonders with your friends.

As you show the images, thoughts will come to your mind of what you did and how you can do better. What are these things? Do you know the proper names or is it just a yellow fish? We have all done this; and, we all feel a little embarrassed when we cannot explain. After all, we are the trained expert and should know these things. Before moving on to the next chapter, I wish to CAUTION you.

Underwater photography is like a strong drug:

- you can never get enough photo equipment
- it keeps costing more and more.

Be proud! You are now an
underwater photographer!!!

CHAPTER 7: PLANNING FOR ONBOARD ENJOYMENT

INTRODUCTION

When on the live aboard, it is immediately obvious who has – and hasn't – planned well for the seven, or ten, days living and diving aboard the ship. The purpose of this chapter is to emphasize the need to plan for activities during the actual time onboard. Planning ahead not only makes the days of "confinement" on the boat more enjoyable, but much easier. The questions to be addressed are:

- What to bring to ensure fun times while onboard? Equipment (basic dive gear, specialized items for detailed tasks, backup), photo stuff (cameras, download capability, laptop, processing software, and printers), and hobbies (books, videos, games, cards),
- What to expect while onboard? Quiet time, group discussions, dive preparation, photo processing, and movies.
- What do you want to accomplish (plenty of time to focus on private objectives)? Better diving skills (night, NITROX, buoyancy control), new experiences (whale sharks, seals, sharks, wreck dives, and volcano hot tubs), research (personal experiences, professional development, environmental "green" contributions to others, fish surveys, etc.), and land tours. [note: bring walking shoes because while on the boat the routine is slip-ons or flip-flops and they will not do for land excursions.]

When offered a chance to climb through the jungle or on an island off the diving areas – definitely take the opportunity to experience the new and exciting. During these times durable shoes are mandatory for coral beaches and rocky hills.

Plan to Bring: As we all recognize, once you leave the dock, access to equipment and supplies is very limited. To ensure that your time onboard is enjoyable, you must start planning early and imaginatively. If you are a novice at underwater photo safaris, you may not recognize and plan for the time available when not diving. The equipment and photographic checklists in the appendix lay out many items that you would think of; however, you must estimate what you would like to accomplish with all of your non-diving time. One answer is obvious – to relax and rest. A very good answer; but, some of us can only do so much resting before we must "do something!" As a result, you must plan for the entire time while you are at sea. The key question is… What do I expect to accomplish while on the boat?

LEISURE TIME EXPECTATION

There will be many opportunities on the boat for quiet time in your cabin or isolated someplace on the boat; plenty of time for dive preparation to include equipment, photography and training; and, plenty of time for group discussions. The chance to spend some excellent reading time is a true pleasure while on vacation. Reading in a concentrated time period enables you to really "get into a book." I usually bring three books for the trip and end up trading for others along the way. In addition to quiet time for yourself, there is plenty of time for you to enjoy the company of others on the boat. You certainly can enjoy time with friends who came along; but, also allow the time and opportunity to enjoy new friendships that will surface during the trip. It is amazing what you learn from others. One unique trait of a die live-aboard is that almost everyone has been diving elsewhere. The stories they tell are marvelous and very important to your future dive trip decisions. On our recent trip to Indonesia aboard the Paradise Dancer, the dive customers had literally been diving in all the oceans (except Antarctica) and most of the seas of the world (such as the Rea Sea and the Black Sea). The stories really help you to consider other locations and adventures. We try to ask – are you going back? This gives you a feel for how they enjoyed their time at these exotic locations. However, whenever anyone asks me the same question, I always answer that the best underwater photo safari is my NEXT one.

Training Time: One of the most effective uses of your time during a multi-day live aboard is to accomplish some type of training. Most dive live aboards have multiple instructors who would love to add to your knowledge and skill levels. Some excellent opportunities relate to:

    Nitrox (enhanced Oxygen)   Night Diving
    Wreck diving Cave Diving
    Master Diver Safety Diver
    Underwater Photography   Photo processing

In addition, you can use the time for individual training such as: computer skills, digital photo processing, camera skills, family album building, language skills, audio tape learning, video lessons, academic courses (self paced), and many others. The key to all these training opportunities is that you must prepare for them. An email to the dive live aboard with your desires will establish if they have an instructor with the necessary skills and equipment to teach your desired topic. Also, if you are going to do individual training, you must bring along the required equipment.

Personal Expectations

As you get ready to depart – and spend all that time with your friends – you need to establish your personal goals for the trip so that you can plan accordingly. There are many concepts for you to develop. Here are some ideas you might consider:

- Improve your **SCUBA** skills: Plan for each dive to be just a little better in the sense of buoyancy and breathing control, sense of safety, and the ability to keep track of your buddy while maximizing your enjoyment of each dive.

- Improve your **photography** skills: This goal is very easy to accomplish as you have as much leisure time as you choose to both take the images and evaluate your successes. Both above water and below water cameras must be understood, played with (in Indonesia, I took over 1,000 images underwater), photos reviewed, and feedback obtained. The good news about traveling with friends is that they WILL give you feedback and critiques.

- Improve your **digital image processing** skills: The beauty of digital photography is that you receive instantaneous feedback on your photos through the screen on the back of your camera. After you correct your settings, you are able to then take multiple photos of the same subject from various angles (if the fish cooperate of course). From there it is a quick download for the fun to start. The skills to view photos on the computer and then "improve" the photos is developed and refined through much practice. As expected, to be able to achieve the goal of improving your digital processing, you must bring along your computer and software packages. Not only must you bring them along, you must open the box, load the programs, and practice prior to departure. This will ensure everything works before becoming isolated on the boat.

- Improve your **fish identification** skills: Several organizations survey fish populations around the world through amateur data taking. The process is fun in that you record the type and number of fish you experience during a dive. The data is then placed on a form and shipped to them. One must be prepared to name the types of fish one sees while diving so the improvement of your knowledge is a good goal for your down time on board. There are plenty of books in the lounge that specialize in the region where you are diving in; but, preparing for the survey while at home prior to the trip will benefit you even more. Perhaps you could download the form on your computer to be shared on the boat.

- **Experience new things**: Of course, the entire underwater photo safari is full of new experiences; but, planning can definitely help increase enjoyment. Some opportunities include land tours, special events, underwater, and cultural experiences.

Special Events on Land

The land tours that are made available during the week of a live aboard are usually outstanding, and special events, such as:

- George the Tortoise: On the Galapagos trip (Sky Dancer), we had multiple land excursions on various islands to investigate the diversity of life that inspired Darwin's theories of evolution so many years ago. On one of those trips, we were shown Lonesome George, a large tortoise who is the last of his species. His species flourished until humans came and loved turtle soup and brought cats who loved the easily found eggs. As a result, he is the last living member of his particular species.

- A village in Papua New Guinea: The tour of a native village in the "outback" of Papua New Guinea was rewarding as we saw how the majority of island people lived. We developed insights into the living conditions which demonstrated the tremendous leap that the developed world has accomplished in the last 200 years.

- Massive Sea Lion: While touring the Galapagos, one land excursion was to walk over to the hill where portions of the movie Master & Commander were filmed. Along the way, we went through a colony of seals, sea lions, and many iguanas (3 feet in length both in and out of the water) on the beach and the rocks. While walking, one of the guests approached a female sea lion too closely; so, the bull charged him. The movement was remarkable in that it was quick, decisive and scary. No harm was done as the guest moved just slightly faster and back to the path. The speed was amazing for a huge ocean going animal. The memory is still vivid of a rapidly moving human escaping his threat to romance between sea lions.

Special Events Underwater

Planning for and equipping for some special underwater events must be accomplished prior to your departure from home. Several items are required that may not occur to you. Some of the special events that have enhanced our trips include:

- Whale Shark Observations: During our time at the distant islands of the Galapagos, there were opportunities to observe and take pictures of some huge whale sharks. The special equipment required for this was a good set of rough gloves to hold onto the rocks as the current sped by and you waited for the whale shark to drift along. In addition, it was very good to take special care concerning depth as the whale shark would gradually descend once it was disturbed by the divers; and, it is not uncommon to notice your depth with surprising expressions – wholly snookers – I am that deep? No way; but, I am coming up now.

- Pygmy Seahorse Hunt: While in Papua New Guinea, we set off looking for the very small pygmy seahorse (size of your small fingernail) in plentiful coral fans. We each searched and searched, but it took the dive leader to know where one stayed. After finding it, we still could not see it as it was too small and in a crevice. We tried to see it just by staring; but, in reality, we needed a magnifying glass. Of course the dive master had one and enabled us to squeeze into the small space and try to identify it. We never saw it! However, we did stick a small point and shoot camera up in the crevice and took many shots of it with one coming out remarkable well.

- Swimming with the Penguins: One of the special events was snorkeling with the Penguins. They are so fast. It was literally true that if one swam past your vision from left to right, you could barely keep your eyes on it. There was no way to focus a camera and take a picture as they were never close and always too fast. If you wanted to take those pictures, you would have to come with a remote control camera setup with an ability to float it near them with you off at a distance.

- Japanese Zero at 30 feet deep: While in Papua New Guinea, a newly discovered aircraft was discussed. It was a pristine World War II Zero in shallow water with easy access. The key was the ability to find it after a long swim underwater. How many of you bring along a compass?

Cultural Events

The cultural events that happen during live aboard adventures are an integral part of the excitement. The offer to mingle in someone else's country, with a boat guide who may even come from that village, is special and should be accepted.

- Water Pump in Bahamas: While on the Wind Dancer, the water pump broke and there was no replacement part; so, the crew had to chase one down. A few of us were asked if we wanted to go ashore on a small island with only a few hundred residents. The short adventure included a small pickup truck holding all six of us, a ride through the small village, a talk with many residents, and finally a ship's water pump at a very unlikely location – an appliance store.

- Head Scarves: One item that is good to bring along is a head scarf. In many countries, dress is part of the custom and insults are easy to stumble into while being ignorant of the issues. While in Indonesia, the offer to go to a Muslin village resulted in a search for head scarves for the ladies.

Chapter 8: The Next Steps

On the Way Home – Prep for Next Trip

After the diving has stopped and you are getting ready to leave the boat and head home, make sure you leverage this great opportunity to prepare for the next trip. While you are thinking about how great your trip has been, and after the last dive, there are things to do. Obviously, washing and drying your dive and camera equipment takes precedence. Usually, after the final dive, the ship must spend a few hours motoring to the departure location. During this time, the wet suit, regulator, BC, and all other equipment should be thoroughly washed in freshwater and laid out to dry in the sun and the wind. Our dive group usually ensures we each start this process early enough to have dry equipment completely packed in our equipment bags prior to final docking. In addition, the photo equipment must be cared for, rinsed, dried and put away in the hand carry luggage for the trip home. While you are doing this, you must check the equipment for any damage and look for items that must be repaired or replaced prior to the next dive excursion. We also like to leave equipment gifts for the staff who treated us well. You would be amazed at how valuable re-chargeable batteries are to the crew that lives on a remote boat and must purchase all items long distance. As a result, we often leave our re-chargeable batteries on the boat with the lead photographer.

After you have finished the physical side of the activity, such as toting and washing the BC's and cameras and then packing them away for transport, move on to the mental side. Sit down in a quiet corner and ask yourself some questions that will help you prepare for the next trip.

- What did I do right?
- What did I do wrong?
- Did I follow the Step Zero process?
- Did I leverage the checklist?
- Did I pack too much
- Did I use everything I packed?
- What should I have left at home?
- What should I have brought?
- Was I sufficiently trained?
- Was I sufficiently in shape?
- Who else should I have invited?

At this point you have transitioned to the point where you are trying to prepare for the next trip. A simple approach could be to pull out the appendix checklist and place an asterisk by essential items as well as comments referencing lessons learned.

Deciding to Go

One of the great pleasures of going on an underwater photo safari is the appreciation of the adventure you have just experienced. While traveling home, or at the cocktail party on the last night on the boat, discussions often break out on how much fun you had and how you want to do it again. It is amazing when the last dinner conversation starts with a huge smile, a wink of the eye, and the question…. Do you remember when I (you/we/the crew/etc) did…..? The fun of reminiscing make that last night on the boat a true pleasure, even realizing that you might not ever see your new best friends again.

As you reminisce about the current adventure your mind naturally turns to the next adventure. Usually it starts with the comment… Well – where to next? What do you have planned? It is amazing when the discussions at dinner morph from the past to the future and almost everyone has a plan. After you have successfully experienced a wonderful underwater photo safari, you naturally want to do it again. The fun is to listen as the various conversations move towards "where to next?" At this point each of us secretly wants to hurry home to our normal lives and families; and then, break away for another great adventure. The decision to go is easy to make.

The questions of when, with whom, and where, usually take some time to solidify. Our dive group, the Rocket Scientists, re-enforces this desire to go by having two or three parties each year focusing on pictures or videos of past trips. Those who went on the last trip talk about the surprises, pleasures, and complexities of the adventure; while the ones who have not been lately wonder… when and where? Each of us either beam with pride while showing the results of our trip or envy the travelers and not so secretly hope that we will be on the next trip. However, to initiate the next step you must make a decision. All the big questions jump out at you:

Where shall we go? Who should we go with? When shall we go?

Beginning Step Zero Again

The beauty of the Step Zero process is that you have just completed a full cycle by going on your first major adventure. As you were returning, you made the decision to go on another underwater photo safari and you are excited all over again. As you know, the first cycle through the Step Zero process enabled you to have confidence when you departed on the trip. This time, you will have confidence early in the process and, through experience, understand all the steps required. You will definitely appreciate the need to follow the checklist.

Yes – You can do It!

*Follow the Step Zero Process
To Have Fun on Another
Underwater Photo Safari*

APPENDIX: UNDERWATER PHOTO SAFARI CHECKLIST[4]

The checklist is divided into two sections.

1. **ACTIONS:** things that you must accomplish. These are decisions and things you the traveler must do.

2. **EQUIPMENT**: a list of things to evaluate you may need on your trip. And, if you decide to you need them, this is a good check list to ensure you have packed them.

Time Periods: These lists have been sorted into "*a time zone*" of WHEN we recommend you accomplish the ACTION or pack the EQUIPMENT. A space is provided to record your progress. If you wait until the last week prior to your SCUBA trip, you will find you won't have enough time to get all the things done.

L = Long time prior to trip (9-12 months); "**Anticipation** Starts"
M = Medium time prior to trip (4-8 months); "**Excitement** Builds"
S = Short time prior to trip (1-3 months); "Excitement **Almost Real**"
LC= Last Chance prior to trip (1-4 weeks); "**Almost There**"

---

[4] **Note:** This list is written for those who will be traveling overseas but works well for those diving in local areas. If an item appears in more than one section it is because it is an important part of the Step Zero process and the way we think. We remind ourselves many times for the same items because we don't want to forget them. This list is for casual diving; however, a good starting point for the more advanced Technical Divers such as those with re-breathers.

IMPORTANT - YOU MUST TAKE THESE FOLLOWING ITEMS!!!!!

Must take dive documents

____ Scuba diving certification cards
____ DAN ID and insurance card
____ NITROX certification card

Must take travel documents

____ Airline Tickets/travel vouchers
____ Dive resort conformation numbers/emails/documents
____ Drivers License
____ Passport
____ Immunization certification
____ Medical insurance card(s)
____ Trip itinerary
____ Visa(s)

Money

____ credit cards (take two or more)
____ lots of cash in all size bills ($100s, $50s, $20s, $10s, $1s)
Take a BUNCH of $1s for tips and small things. Merchants don't make change in remote places. Your arrival airport is usually a good place to change some your larger bills onto local currency. Don't rely on ATMS but use ATMS if available.

These are ACTIONS you must do

Long-Term Actions " Anticipation Starts"

L _____ take leave/vacation from work
L _____ luggage catch up days: add them to your travel plan, some luggage will get lost on the airlines and a rest day will give it a chance to catch up with you.
L _____ make airline reservations
L _____ make **hotel** reservations
L _____ make dive resort reservations
L _____ passport expiration date; check it and ensure you will have at least 6 months left when you enter your vacation area, more is better
L _____ read lessons learned from your last trip
L _____ rest days, put them in your travel plan. This will give your body a chance to catch up and for you to see the local area and enjoy your trip
L _____ time zones, do you cross the international date line? Watch this, you can lose or gain one day; this can screw up your travel plans if you don't plan.
L _____ Dive trip planning parties; get together with friends and discuss going on a trip; medium term parties will check individual progress and provide group support

Medium-Term Actions "Excitement Builds"

M _____ arrange care for animals/pets/lawn/flowers while you are away
M _____ boat, determine if will you diving be from large boats with nice ladders or from small dive tenders with small or no ladders.
M _____ boat, your body, are you physically fit to climb into and out of small dive tenders
M _____ boat, photo facilities, will there be a camera table and rinse tank
M _____ boat, human facilities, will there be a changing room and bathroom
M _____ charge rechargeable batteries prior to trip; let sit for 20 days; test and check for batteries that have discharged; a discharge battery indicates a week battery; toss it out and replace it with a known/tested good battery
M _____ check all O-rings on lights and cameras

M	____	customs and import restrictions for the countries you visit and the US, understand what they are and be ready to comply
M	____	dive trip planning parties; get together and check individual progress. This will provide support and motivation to all in the travel group.
M	____	diving conditions, what is the water temperature, do I need a wet suit, the thickness of our hood, gloves, and wet suit
M	____	diving conditions, dive depth, will you be doing shallow, wall, reef or wreck diving
M	____	diving conditions, will the current be still or strong drift diving
M	____	diving conditions, will the seas be rough open water or calm, sheltered diving
M	____	diving conditions, will you be shore diving
M	____	diving conditions, read the reviews in the magazines and in the on line news groups
M	____	diving equipment rentals, does the dive shop rent equipment, do you need to reserve it
M	____	diving level, what skill level is required, beginner, intermediate, experienced, or professional
M	____	diving, are there training courses I can take
M	____	diving, are there training courses I need
M	____	check your electrical devices to see if they are compatible with the electricity in the area you are going or transiting
M	____	check electrical voltage and wall plug design for each county and ship you will visit or be on; verify, it may change in the same country, find out what they are and read the power supply on your equipment; will it work; do I need a plug adaptor
M	____	plug adaptors, what kind(s) do I need
M	____	plug adaptors, how many do I need (two minimum, one for room and one for charging table)
M	____	entertainment in the local area, tours, shopping, museums, parks, music, food, farming, golf, site seeing; get out and see the local area
M	____	get Divers Alert Network (DAN) scuba diving insurance
M	____	get necessary shots/vaccinations/prescriptions (malaria, tetanus, Hep A&B, polio . . .)
M	____	buy new equipment
M	____	test new equipment
M	____	have regulator serviced

M	____	check your regulator after it is serviced (we have seen may regulators that were serviced just prior to the trip but NOT checked. And then were found to NOT function at the vacation location.)
M	____	insurance, do get overseas medical, scuba diving and medical evacuation insurance
M	____	insurance, should I get lost luggage or canceled trip Insurance
M	____	local area, get maps of where you are going; This will greatly improve you enjoyment by knowing where you, are going and have been
M	____	local history and culture, buy books and read them. You will enjoy a lot more of what you see on the trip
M	____	local tour organization/hotel/resort/dive outfits, what is their reputation? Check on line and in magazines
M	____	luggage, number of pieces, check with airlines for how many you may check and carry on
M	____	luggage weight restrictions, understand what they areso you won't be caught with overweight charges
M	____	luggage size restrictions, if you bag is too big, you will have to check it. Many small airlines (island hoppers) have almost no overhead storage. If your bag is very large and/or heavy the airline will not check it or may charge a fee
M	____	make copy of medical prescriptions (take with you)
M	____	make copy of optical prescription (take with you)
M	____	make list of contact(s) phone numbers you may need to call (family, friends and work to tell them you arrived safely, may be late returning or not returning at all)
M	____	reconfirm all hotel reservations
M	____	reconfirm all resort reservations
M	____	reconfirm dive operation arrangements
M	____	safety, what are the local diving safety requirement, do you need special equipment
M	____	test all lights
M	____	test regulator on spare tank; a test dive with the regulator is best

Short-Term Actions "Excitement Almost Real"

S ____ alcohol, tobacco, foods, alcohol, what products can you import into or out of the places you will visit

S ____ diving gas, does the resort have NITROX

S ____ fishing restrictions, what can you do in the vacation area, pole fishing, spear fishing or none

S ____ food and organic imports, what can you take into or out of the places you will visit

S ____ food, tell the resorts if you have any special food or diet needs

S ____ keep packaging for all medications to show customs inspectors (plain pills in a plastic bag with no packaging may get confiscated because it cannot be identified as being legitimate)

S ____ internet, is there internet in your vacation area at the hotel/resort/café so you may send emails to your friends at work and tell them how much fun you are having on vacation

S ____ label everything; keeps it from getting mixed up on boat (we use white electrical tape and a black water proof market)

S ____ do NOT buy new equipment at the last minute. You will NOT have enough time to test and verify its proper operation

S ____ do NOT have you regulator serviced just prior to your trip. You won't have time to verify its proper operation

S ____ check dive computer battery/change if you have doubt

S ____ lay out all dive equipment from head to foot to make certain you have all of it.

S ____ after you do the above check, pack it

S ____ lay out all camera equipment is its proper place to make certain you have it all; hook it all up and check operation (this will show you have all the parts)

S ____ after you do the above check, pack it.

S ____ pack fragile photo gear in cloths, makes good use of your cloths

S ____ take photo of your packed camera bag and suitcase showing the contents and put on your computer (good reference when repacking, seems like the suitcases are smaller on the way back)

S ____ hand carry one small UW P&S camera; this way if your check UW camera gets lost you will at least one UW camera for the duration of your vacation

S	____	luggage, mark luggage with colored tape or string; makes it easy to find in the airport and hotel (we use stripes of duct tape, easy to see and no one else uses it)
S	____	do NOT put photo stickers or logos on photo cases, it marks them as expensive, good to steel
S	____	luggage, put two name tags on each piece, they tend to get ripped off
S	____	luggage, take an extra, empty folding, very, very light duffle bag to hold the treasures you will by on the trip
S	____	hand carry all photo equipment if you can
S	____	if you must check a pelican photo case, put it in a cheep duffle bag to disguise it
S	____	make copies of your C-cards, passport, visas and other papers (swap with travel buddy)
S	____	money in local area; what kind to they use, how do you convert, do they have ATMs, WHERE can you do it, do they take credit card (checks are almost never used overseas)
S	____	pack everything in plastic bags, keeps it dry and easy to sort; you can then put the plastic bags in your room and put your suitcase in the boat bulk storage
S	____	pack liquids in plastic bags, they all leak and you don't want the lotions, shampoos and mouth washes to get on your cloths
S	____	pack only SMALL travel sizes of toiletries; you won't need a two months supply, large sizes are heavy; go buy small sizes just for your trip.
S	____	place like things (like photo cables) in the same small plastic bag; makes search for items easy and small items won't get hidden under the big stuff you are not looking for
S	____	pack things with dangling cables in plastic bags; keeps things from getting all tangled or being torn out and broken; the jungle you have in your carry on bag can be tamed by putting things in plastic bags; the searching and extracting is a lot easier
S	____	make a list of the phone numbers and emails of the resorts and tour companies you are going to visit so you can take on trip and call them if necessary
S	____	give a copy of the list of phone numbers and emails of the resorts and tour companies you are going to visit to your family and friends at home so they can contact you
S	____	make list of the folks at home and get their phone numbers and emails so you can call them (and maybe tell them you will not be returning)

- S ____ phone service in your vacation area, is there service, (in some remote areas, there is NO phone service)
- S ____ phone service, will you cell phone work in the vacation area
- S ____ plants, arrange for someone to take care of your plants, again
- S ____ plants, what can you take into or out of the places you visit; verify agricultural restrictions
- S ____ reconfirm all airline reservations and seat assignments
- S ____ refill medical prescriptions (we cannot stress this enough)
- S ____ reconfirm all hotel reservations
- S ____ reconfirm all resort reservations
- S ____ reconfirm dive operation arrangements
- S ____ smoking restrictions, what are the guidelines for the hotels, resorts, and dive boats you will visiting/using/staying
- S ____ smoking restrictions, will you be traveling with smokers or non-smokers - be considerate
- S ____ smoking, what quantity of tobacco can you take into or out of the places you will visit
- S ____ sharpen all knifes and lightly coat with oil
- S ____ State Department, check their web site for current information on the local political situation; are there a cautions or travel advisories
- S ____ State Department, get location and contact information of the local US Embassy services
- S ____ State Department, register your overseas trip with state department, important for remote and unstable political areas
- S ____ TSA, get, print and read all TSA luggage rules
- S ____ TSA, get, print and read all Airline luggage rules
- S ____ stop home snail mail, newspapers and deliveries
- S ____ tell neighbors you are going, AGAIN,
- S ____ give them your contact info, AGAIN
- S ____ get/verify their contact info, AGAIN
- S ____ tipping expectations, research what is expected, what is too much, what is the norm, how do you tip, what currency do you use, can you use credit card
- S ____ write down CC numbers and international phone numbers to call CC companies

S	____	pack ONLY needed items; not all that you own;
S	____	do NOT over pack
S	____	weigh luggage; repack or toss out stuff if you are too heavy
*S	____	take copies of the wavers you sent in advance and give to boat (this will save you from filling them out again, forms tend to get lost)
*S	____	Diver certification cards; DO YOU HAVE THEM!!
*S	____	Passport, do you have it!!!!!
*S	____	go to your luggage and toss out 10 pounds of stuff, you packed too much!!!

Last Chance "Almost There"

LC	____	call credit card companies, tell them you are going overseas so they may adjust your spending profile
LC	____	get necessary pills (prescriptions, over the counter, malaria, vitamins, . .)
LC	____	pets, implement your plan for someone to take care of your pets or take them to a pet boarding facility
LC	____	reconfirm all airline reservations and seat assignments
LC	____	stop home snail mail, newspapers and deliveries
LC	____	tell neighbors you are going, AGAIN,
LC	____	give them your contact info, AGAIN
LC	____	get/verify their contact info, AGAIN
*LC	____	Diver certification cards; DO YOU HAVE THEM!!
*LC	____	Passport, do you have it!!!!!
*LC	____	go to your luggage and **toss out** 10 pounds of stuff, you packed too much!!!

ACTION THINGS TO DO ON THE TRIP

*	____	When you arrive, call your dive tour company and let them know you have arrived in the vacation area and will be at the appropriate location for pick up as scheduled.
	____	buy things for your trip book; maps, photos & postcards
	____	get list of your dive sites
	____	get list of the other passengers on your dive boat, resort and hotels

- _____ keep activity list and opinions for reference. At the end of the cruse/stay you may wish to write a performance critique or provide feedback to the boat and or hotel; positive feedback is also appreciated
- _____ make list of things you need for your next trip
- _____ make list of things you DIDN'T use on the trip, do NOT take them next trip; unused items are just dead weight that displaces items you could have used
- _____ notify your home family or neighbors of your travel progress during your trip; they want to know you are ok
- _____ purchases, make list of what you buy and so you can put on customs list when you reenter the US *(see US Customs and Boarder Protection CBP Publication No. 0000-00512)*
- _____ purchases, mail or ship your treasures home, saves dragging them trough the airport and keeps you within the airline weight limits
- _____ purchases, do NOT fancy wrap your purchases, you will have to unwrap them and show them to customs; wait until you are home to gift wrap your treasures
- _____ start lessons learned list

ACTION THINGS TO DO AT THE END OF THE TRIP

- _____ buy replacement or upgrade to better equipment
- _____ did you have all the correct power plugs
- _____ did you have all the correct diving papers, certification cards, visas, . . .
- _____ did you have enough cash money
- _____ did you have enough spare luggage to carry home all the things you bought
- _____ did your credit cards work
- _____ fix broken equipment
- _____ lessons learned, make a list of what went well and not-well so you can use it for your next trip
- _____ lessons learned, write them down
- _____ make a list of what you FORGOT and put it on your check list and lessons learned for next year.
- _____ make a list of what you took TOO much of, clothing, tools, cameras, electronics, paper, books, . . . and put in your check list and lessons learned for next year

____ make a trip book to show your friends, photos, videos, maps, souvenir tickets and such
____ make list of what broke and get it fixed
____ make list of what was depleted and get replenish NOW for your next trip (suntan lotion, mask defog . . .)
____ replace lost or broken equipment
____ send "thank you" notes to boat crew, hotels and friends you made on the trip

ACTION THINGS TO NOT TAKE ON THE TRIP

____ illegal drugs, do NOT take them; foreign laws are very tough and the jails are not nice
____ scuba tanks, they are very heavy and provided by most scuba operations as part of your dive charter
____ weights, they are very heavy and provided by most scuba operations as part of your dive charter
____ heavy books, take paperbacks and swap books with others on the trip; use the local take one, leave one library (consider taking one of the new "Electronic Book Readers" such as the Sony book reader of the Amazon Kindle)
____ food, most items are prohibited and seized at customs when entering a country, buy local; remember, you are on an adventure, try something new
____ too many cloths; use items that can be cleaned in your room on the trip or use hotel laundry
____ large containers of liquids; they are heavy, use travel sizes or buy local
____ you may want to rent heavy regulators or BCs from your dive operation; saves a LOT of luggage weight.
____ do NOT take jewelry or valuable show-off items on you trip; they will become a target for the local thief
____ do NOT take your personal check book. Personal checks are almost NEVER accepted.

Equipments Check List

The list is segmented by the type of equipment and by time zone. Many of the items require significant lead time to acquire. Go get them or locate them in your house and put them into a "take on the trip PILE", start early. Yep, a "pile" may sound stupid but it works. Put everything you want to take into one, out of the way place and keep adding to it so you won't forget the item. When you're your mind thinks of something to take, get up right then and go get it and put it in the pile. Or, make note of what to get and put the note in the pile. Or, remove an item from the pile so you won't take too much.

<u>Dive Equipment</u>

Basic Equipment

- ____ **M**-buoyancy compensation device
- ____ **M**-dive bag, mesh for carrying all this stuff into the boat
- ____ **M**-dive boots
- ____ **M**-dive computer
- ____ **M**-dive knife
- ____ **M**-dive long book with sufficient blank pages
- ____ **M**-dive mask
- ____ **M**-dry bag for keeping your dry towel and shirt dry on the dive boat
- ____ **M**-ear wash
- ____ **M**-fins
- ____ **M**-mask defog solution
- ____ **M**-regulator with submersible pressure gauge and octopus
- ____ **M**-retractors for small equipment (lights and such)
- ____ **M**-save-a-dive kit (spare mask strap, fin strap, regulator mouthpiece)
- ____ **M**-snorkel
- ____ **M**-strong plastic box to put you eyeglasses and such into while you are diving; keeps them from getting broken or lost
- ____ **M**-custom, padded weight belt (the boat will provide standard belts)
- ____ **M**-wet suit (two are better, one warm and one warmer; vest, shorty)
- ____ **M**-white electrical tame and marking pen to mark equipment

Safety Equipment

____ **M**-chemical/cyalume light stick
____ **M**-dive alert air horn (connects to the regulator, very loud)
____ **M**-Divers Alert Network (DAN) scuba diving insurance
____ **M**-travel insurance
____ **M**-inflatable safety sausage (easy to see you from the boat and dive tenders and to find other divers on surface)
____ **M**-signaling mirror
____ **M**-UW strobe light for personal use
____ **M**-whistle

Backup Equipment

____ **M**-dive boots
____ **M**-dive light
____ **M**-2nd dive knife
____ **M**-dive slate
____ **M**-2nd dry box/bag
____ **M**-fins
____ **M**-gloves
____ **M**-hose clips, attached hoses to BC
____ **M**-mask (really consider this, mask are really personal)
____ **M**-octo regulator keepers
____ **M**-regulator
____ **M**-stainless steel clip rings

Photography

L-Land Camera *(are you going to take one)*
____ **M**-batteries and extra batteries
____ **M**-lots of business cards-for land work
____ **M**-charger for land camera battery

- ____ **M**-extra lenses (wide angle/telephoto)
- ____ **M**-land camera, prime use, DSLR
- ____ **M**-land camera, spare use, P&S
- ____ **M**-small tripod
- ____ **M**-model release (see page 71 for more info)
- ____ **M**-Completed US Customs Form 4457 for registering and getting your expensive, professional photo equipment in and out of customs
- ____ **M**-lots of camera memory cards
- ____ **M**-NON-photo bag for taking cameras on land tours, photo bags draw too much attention and say steal me
- ____ **S**-air blower for cleaning camera
- ____ **S**-camera brush
- ____ **S**-lens caps
- ____ **S**-lens filters (polarizer, UV filter, neutral density and such)
- ____ **S**-lens hoods
- ____ **S**-lens cleaning paper
- ____ **S**-micro fiber towel

L-Under Water (UW) camera (are you going to take one)

- ____ **M**-batteries and extra batteries
- ____ **M**-lots of business cards-for UW work
- ____ **M**-charger for UW camera battery
- ____ **M**-desiccant packs (go into the underwater housing for your camera and removes moisture to reduce fogging)
- ____ **M**-extra lenses (wide angle/macro)
- ____ **M**-UW camera, prime use, DSLR
- ____ **M**-UW camera, spare use, P&S
- ____ **M**-lots of camera memory cards
- ____ **M**-UW camera housing, prime use
- ____ **M**-UW camera housing, spare use
- ____ **M**-UW focus/modeling light
- ____ **M**-UW strobes with cords
- ____ **M**-UW strobe arms

____ **M**-model release (see page 71 for more info)
____ **M**-Completed US Customs Form 4457 for registering and getting your expensive, professional photo equipment in and out of customs

Lights

____ **M**-batteries for all lights (count and check size for what you need)
____ **M**-dive lights (prime, small, backup)
____ **M**-small flashlight for searching in cary on bag
____ **M**-small light for room/ night light
____ **M**-spare bulbs for all lights
____ **M**-UW strobe light
____ **M**-UW tank marker light
____ **M**-consider taking the new LED lights now coming onto the market. They produce good light, are very easy on battery life, and the LEDs last a long time when compared to the old glass bulbs
____ **S**-extra batteries
____ **S**-extra lights
____ **S**-extra O-rings for lights

Batteries

____ **M**-batteries for all cameras (determine sizes and number needed)
____ **M**-batteries for all lights (determine sizes and number needed)
____ **M**-batteries for nose reduction headphones
____ **M**-batteries for cell phone
____ **M**-batteries for GPS
____ **M**-battery tester (a good cheep tester from Radio Shack works fine $5)
____ **M**-extra batteries (all needed sizes)
____ **M**-extra batteries for all dive computers
____ **M**-chargers for all the above
____ **M**-small battery tester

Repair Tools

- ____ **M**-crescent wrench
- ____ **M**-dental tape and large needles
- ____ **M**-double end brass clip
- ____ **M**-duct tape
- ____ **M**-extra burst-plugs for tanks (unique item, not needed in most places)
- ____ **M**-flame maker for burning end of nylon cords (don't take on plane/ buy at location)
- ____ **M**-knife sharpening tool/stone
- ____ **M**-leather man tool
- ____ **M**-multi-purpose dive tool
- ____ **M**-nylon cables ties, small and large (zip ties)
- ____ **M**-plastic bags, several sizes
- ____ **M**-rubber bands
- ____ **M**-rubberized repair tape
- ____ **M**-screwdrivers, several sizes and very small (for photo equipment)
- ____ **M**-screwdrivers (blade, Philips and Terex)
- ____ **M**-single edge razor blades for cutting things
- ____ **M**-small battery tester
- ____ **M**-small, medium, large bungee cords
- ____ **M**-spare LP and HP plugs for regulator 1st stage and wrenches to fit
- ____ **M**-spare LP and HP swivels for regulator
- ____ **M**-super glue
- ____ **M**-surgical tubing
- ____ **M**-swiss army knife
- ____ **M**-tire patch kit to fix BCD
- ____ **M**-velcro ties
- ____ **M**-WD-40, small, don't take on airplane, by at location
- ____ **M**-small brass brush, good for cleaning electrical contacts
- ____ **S**-swabs, good for cleaning tight spots
- ____ **S**-plastic bags to put things in; keeps stuff from getting tangled/lost

O-rings (very light and essential so take many spares)

____ **M**-extra O-rings for everything (lights, camera, strobe sync cables, regulator, LP and HP connector hoses, tank O-rings . . . .)
____ **M**-extra O-rings for UW camera housings
____ **M**-silicone grease for O-rings, (watch for manufacture recommendations to use specific grease, follow them)
____ **M**-dental tooth scraper tool to extract tough O-rings
____ **M**-plastic O-ring tool to get O-rings off and out of equipment

Books & Owner's Manuals

____ **M**-most manuals are available in electronic formant, get them
____ **M**-put the electronic manuals on your computer, it saves space and weight
____ **M**-Air/NITROX tables
____ **M**-area travel & tourist books
____ **M**-Electronic book reader, consider taking one of the new "Electronic Book Readers" such as the Sony book reader of the Amazon Kindle. The can contain MANY books for your reading pleasure and are very easy to carry
____ **M**-land camera owner's manual
____ **M**-dive computer owner's manual (this is IMPORTANT)
____ **M**-fish ID books (the boat usually has a good set)
____ **M**-GPS owner's manual
____ **M**-how to books for (photography, fish ID, bird ID, .)
____ **M**-maps, local and area
____ **M**-UW strobe owner's manual
____ **M**-UW camera owner's manual
____ **M**-owner's manual for EVERYTHING you take

First Aid Kit

____ **M**-travel medial kit, make one and put these things in it; use a clear plastic bag; easy to pack and see what's in the bag

- S-alcohol wash for ears
- S-antiseptic cream/lotion
- S-antibiotics
- S-anti-sting lotion for sea urchin and jelly fish stings
- S-aspirin and other pain relievers
- S-band aids
- S-bug repellant, pack light, use stick or wipes
- S-cough drops
- S-decongestant
- S-pooper starter
- S-pooper stopper
- S-sunscreen

Medical and Personal Health

- M-determine surface and water temperature where you are going (determines wet suit needs)
- M-determine altitude at which you will be diving, sea level or mountain lake (determines decompression constraints)
- M-special medical equipment (parts for prosthetic limbs, . .)
- M-diabetes blood/sugar test equipment
- M-get divers Alert Network (DAN) scuba diving medical insurance
- M-get physical certifying you are medically certified to scuba dive; be honest with yourself. THIS IS A BIG DEAL
- M-get travel insurance for delays, lost luggage, . . .
- M-get medial insurance for traveling in remote areas (DAN has good coverage options which include scuba diving)
- M-malaria pills if required
- M-special inoculations for area you are going (Hepatitis A&B, Typhoid, tetanus, polio, influenza)
- M-pack sufficient prescription medications for duration of trip plus extra days, THIS IS IMPORTANT
- M-copies of written prescription to show customs

- ____ **S**-antibacterial wipes
- ____ **S**-dental hygiene (tooth brush/paste, floss, picks, mouth wash . .)
- ____ **S**-deodorant
- ____ **S**-diabetes blood sugar test kit
- ____ **S**-fungus lotions
- ____ **S**-hand cream/lotion
- ____ **S**-non-prescription medications
- ____ **S**-prescription medications for duration of trip, again, THIS IS IMPORTANT
- ____ **S**-original packing for all medications, prescription and over the counter; customs officials may confiscate any pills/medications that cannot be identified
- ____ **S**-copies of written prescription to show customs
- ____ **S**-razor and shaving cream
- ____ **S**-unmentionable items
- ____ **S**-washing lotions for body and cloths
- ____ **S**-bug spray
- ____ **S**-sun glasses, polarized, reduces water glare
- ____ **S**-suntan lotion
- ____ **S**-sea sick pills
- ____ **S**-chap stick

Clothing

- ____ **M**-plastic bags, for putting cloths in and keeping them dry and clean/dirty
- ____ **M**-BIG plastic Zip Locking bag (4-5 gallon) to use as a dry-bag to put your towel or shirt into while you are diving. (it is really handy when you are on a day boat to keep a few things dry. These are cheaper than a commercial dry bag and work just as well.
- ____ **S**-Bathing suit(s)
- ____ **S**-beach robe/skirt
- ____ **S**-blouses/shirts
- ____ **S**-clothesline and clips (make out of nylon cord and two carabineers for use on boat dive deck, hang bathing suits to day)
- ____ **S**-hat, with chin strap so it won't blow off, needed for sun

____ S-polo shirt
____ S-sandals, rubber, for working along the beach or in the water or getting in and out of boats when you go ashore to explore a remote island
____ S-walking shorts
____ S-skirt
____ S-socks
____ S-tennis shoes
____ S-trousers
____ S-T-shirts
____ S-underclothing

Personal Items

____ M-eye contacts
____ M-extra pair of eye contacts
____ M-eye glasses
____ M-extra pair of eye glasses
____ M-sun glasses
____ M-extra pair of sun glasses
____ M-reading glasses
____ M-TSA approved locks for checked and hand luggage & photo cases
____ S-binoculars
____ S-business cards
____ S-E-books for your Kindle or Sony E-book reader
____ S-small travel alarm clock for room
____ S-eye contact solution and case
____ S-DVDs to watch
____ S-extra luggage bag for taking things home
____ S-hair bands
____ S-paper copies of your scuba certification cards, put in your luggage and with your passport
____ S-pens, pencils and paper
____ S-3x5 cards

____ S-reading material (try to buy/exchange locally, saves weight)
____ S-rubber doorstop, put under your room door to hold it closed
____ S-steel cable to lock you luggage to a pole/bed/chair
____ S-sewing kit with needle and various threads
____ S-big needle and carpet thread for sewing equipment
____ S-tote bags, small and large

Personal Computer

____ M-computer for processing photos, email, watching movies, writing notes, keeping a dive log, logging GPS data of you dive sites
____ M-computer battery charger
____ M-external HD for backing up computer data
____ M-camera memory card reader
____ M-several thumb drives
____ M-Software (SW) for burning CDs and DVDs
____ M-SW for sending emails
____ M-SW for processing photos
____ M-SW for word processing
____ S-blank CDs and DVDs
____ S-CD/DVD protector sleeves
____ S-pen to write on CDs and DVDs
____ S-Form-4457 to get your computer in/out of the countries; this is important and very necessary to prove ownership and country of origination for expensive equipments; If you don't have this form, you may spend a lot of time proving you own the equipment and are not trying to sell the equipment
____ S-list of important URLs for quick reference

Other Personal Electronics

____ M-cables for computer, iPod and camera to display photos/video on TV (watch format, is it PAL or NSTC)
____ M-cables to connect all your things together

- ____ **M**-cell phone w/authorization for international calls & charger
- ____ **M**-pre-paid international calling card keyed to the area where you are traveling
- ____ **M**-battery chargers for everything electronic
- ____ **M**-external speaker for computer/iPod; makes room listening easier
- ____ **M**-iPod with charger
- ____ **M**-PDA with security protection
- ____ **M**-satellite telephone with charger
- ____ **M**-short wave radio; excellent for current events in remote locations
- ____ **S**-access codes and dialing instructions for your cell phone while in the countries you'll be visiting and for the local telephones in the countries you visit
- ____ **S**-ear bud headphones
- ____ **S**-electrical plug style adaptor so you can pug in at travel location; take more than one so you can charge in more than one room (cabin, camera room and battery charging station
- ____ **S**-extension cords (two, one for battery charging station and one for room) that are thin, light and have multiple plug openings
- ____ **S**-flash light and night light for room
- ____ **S**-GPS to plot and record travel locations and dive sites
- ____ **S**-noise reduction headphones (great for very long airplane trips)
- ____ **S**-do NOT pack spare Lithium batteries in your check luggage. The batteries may be a fire hazard. TSA says they must be had carried in individual plastic/insulated cases.

www.ingramcontent.com/pod-product-compliance
Lightning Source LLC
Chambersburg PA
CBHW041118300426
44112CB00002B/17